Inspired
THE FLEMING COLLECTION
Celebrating Ten Years of The Fleming-Wyfold Art Foundation

THE FLEMING COLLECTION

Published by the
Trustees of The Fleming-Wyfold Art Foundation, 2010
with texts from two exhibitions at
The Fleming Collection
13 Berkeley Street, London W1J 8DU
www.flemingcollection.co.uk

Inspired: Forty Years of Collecting Scottish Art
8 July – 30 August 2008
Inspired Part II: Scottish Art From The Fleming Collection
7 July – 5 September 2009

ISBN 0-9545137-7-0

Editors: Lucia Lindsay and Tim Cornwell
Exhibition organisers: Lucia Lindsay and Tim Cornwell

Designed and typeset in Eagle and Bembo by Briony Anderson and Flit, London
Printed by Empress Litho, London

Front Cover: George Leslie Hunter (1877–1931) *Peonies in a Chinese Vase* © FWAF

The proceeds from the sale of this book go towards supporting The Fleming Collection.
For a complete list of current publications, please contact The Fleming Collection.

The Fleming Collection is supported by The Fleming-Wyfold Art Foundation
Registered charity no.1080197

CONTENTS

INSPIRED

WORKS FROM THE FLEMING COLLECTION

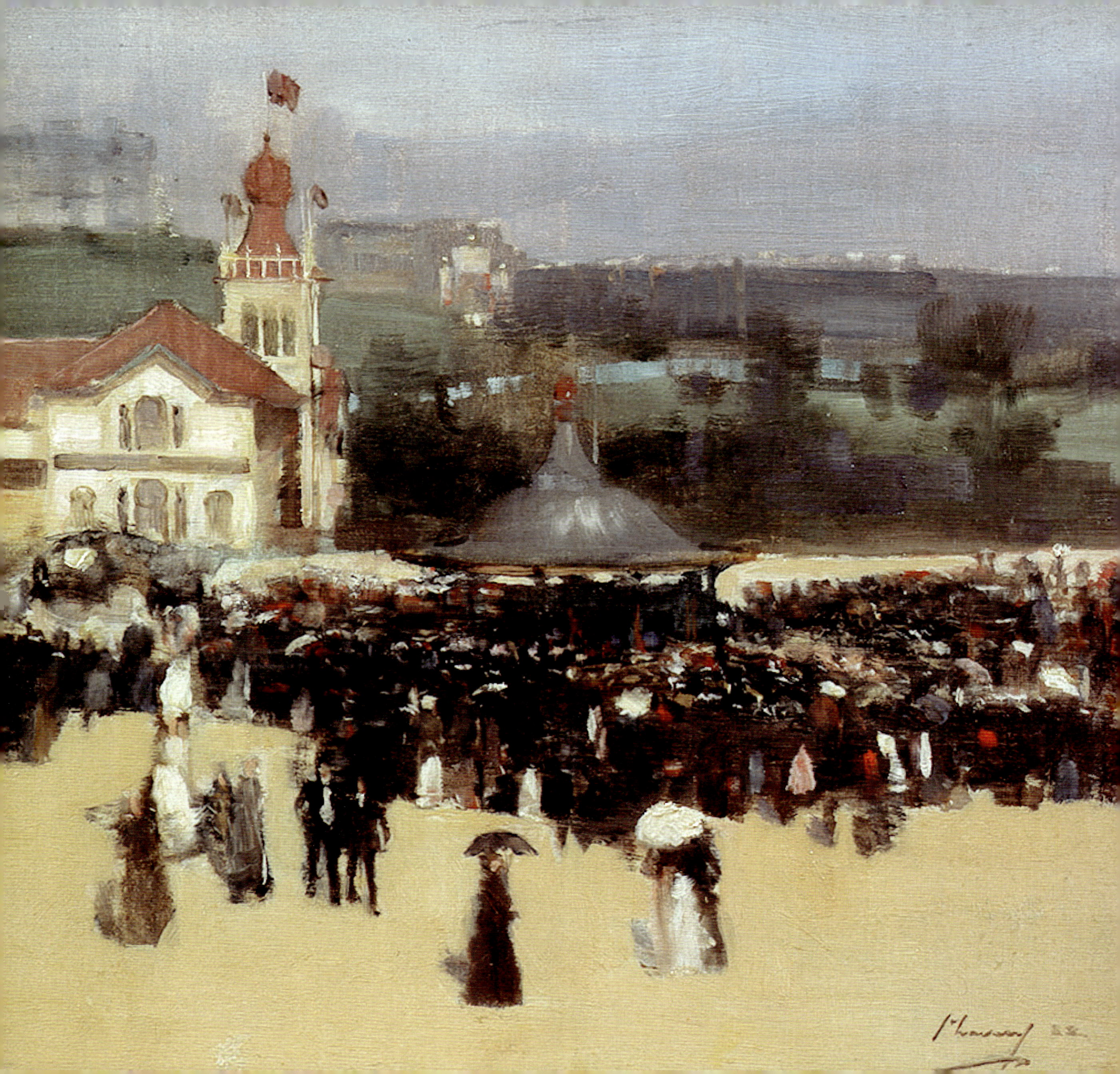

FOREWORD

Inspired is a celebration of the impact that works of art have on the viewer and the brilliant creative responses that can be drawn from them. The passages in this publication have been selected from two past exhibitions at The Fleming Collection, London, for which some of today's leading lights from the worlds of culture and business selected their favourite work from the permanent collection and wrote about it.

2010 is an exciting year as it marks the tenth anniversary of The Fleming-Wyfold Art Foundation. Since The Foundation was established as a registered charity in 2000 the aim has been to further understanding in Scottish art through a changing exhibition programme at The Fleming Collection gallery. The gallery, which is open to the public free of charge, exhibits works from the permanent collection and other public and private collections of Scottish paintings and is now recognised as 'an embassy for Scottish Art'.

We are grateful to the participants for their thoughtful contributions and to Lucia Lindsay and Tim Cornwell for their work on this project. We wish to thank Flemings Hotel, Mayfair and General Manager, Simon Scarborough for their sponsorship and Fleming Family & Partners Ltd for being supporting sponsors of the publication. The Scotsman has been extremely generous working with The Fleming Collection as media partner and in allowing us to reproduce many photographs from their archive.

Robin Fleming, Chairman of Trustees, Selina Skipwith, Keeper of Art
The Fleming-Wyfold Art Foundation

Chosen by Andrew Patrick
Former Director of
The Fine Art Society,
London, Collector
The Blue Hungarians
1888, oil on canvas
Sir John Lavery RA RSA
(1856–1941)

SPONSOR'S FOREWORD

Flemings Hotel was established by Robert Fleming who was born in Farnham, Surrey in 1820. His training as a valet to the Marquis and Marchioness of Angelsey at 1 Old Burlington Street in London, may have provided the ideal experience for running a high class hotel. Post Office Directories show that Fleming acquired Nos. 9 and 10 Half Moon Street and No. 41 Clarges Street between 1852 and 1883. Dating from 1730, Half Moon Street remained a very good address in Fleming's day, the home of nobility, surgeons, physicians, a barrister and an attorney. Its name was derived from the *Half Moon* public house on the corner where James Boswell lodged in 1768.

Though history does not relate whether a connection exists between our founder and Robert Fleming, founder of Flemings bank, since The Fleming Collection opened its doors to the public nearby in 2002 we have been extremely proud to sponsor publications such as this and to support some remarkable exhibitions.

Today the six interconnecting Georgian townhouses which make up Flemings Hotel's rooms, suites and apartments in Mayfair, cleverly fuse the traditional charm and elegance of the Georgian period with contemporary style. We welcome guests visiting The Fleming Collection to experience the luxury of staying at Flemings and to enjoy the eccentric glamour of The Front Room, opulence of The Cocktail & Tea Rooms and exquisite modern cuisine at Flemings Grill.

Simon Scarborough, General Manager, Flemings Hotel, Mayfair, Est. 1851

INTRODUCTION

The *Inspired* exhibitions have generated a snapshot of contemporary responses to works of art in The Fleming Collection. The people who have written passages about the artworks that inspire them – along with the pictures themselves – reflect a small cross-section of Scotland's rich cultural heritage, from art, to music, to literature. The Fleming Collection has always lent paintings to museums and galleries and been used for research by curators, many of whom are contributors.

Musicians from a broad range of genres have linked their own compositions or performances to their chosen painting. Recent collaborations with playwrights and musicians have resulted in new works including *Scottish Miniatures* at The Cheltenham Music Festival in 2006 and a play by The Clamjamfry Company in 2007. Poet Jen Hadfield has based her poem, written for this exhibition, on Alasdair Wallace's painting *Flock of Birds*. Frequently set design and painting overlap and inform one another, as illustrated here by director David McVicar and film producer Andrew Macdonald.

It should be acknowledged that without the passion of the Collection's Trustees and Keepers (David Donald, Bill Smith and Selina Skipwith) and the support of the Fleming family, this independent and invaluable resource for Scottish art would not exist.

Tim Cornwell, Arts Correspondent, The Scotsman
Lucia Lindsay, Assistant Keeper of Art,
The Fleming-Wyfold Art Foundation

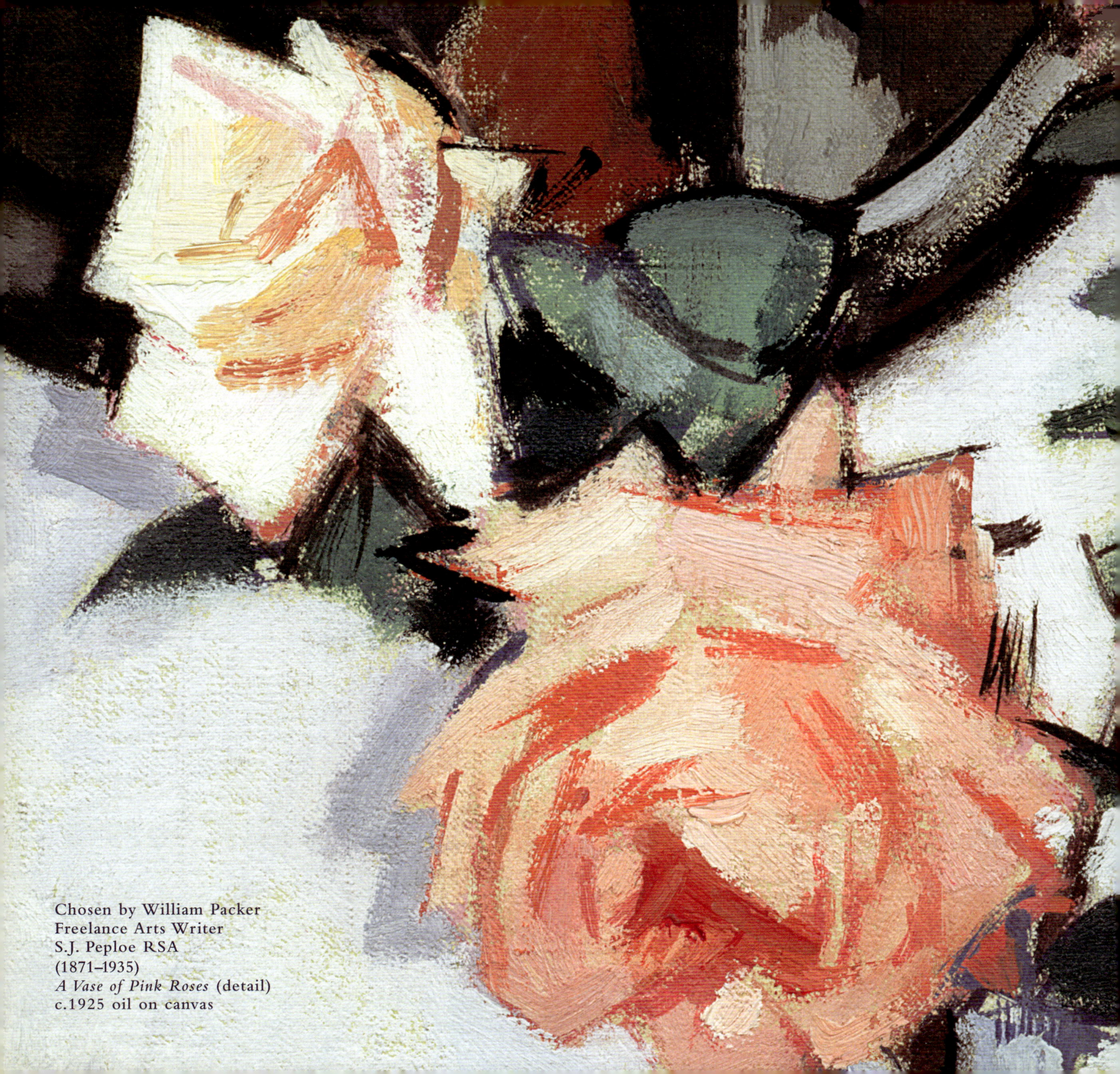

Chosen by William Packer
Freelance Arts Writer
S.J. Peploe RSA
(1871–1935)
A Vase of Pink Roses (detail)
c.1925 oil on canvas

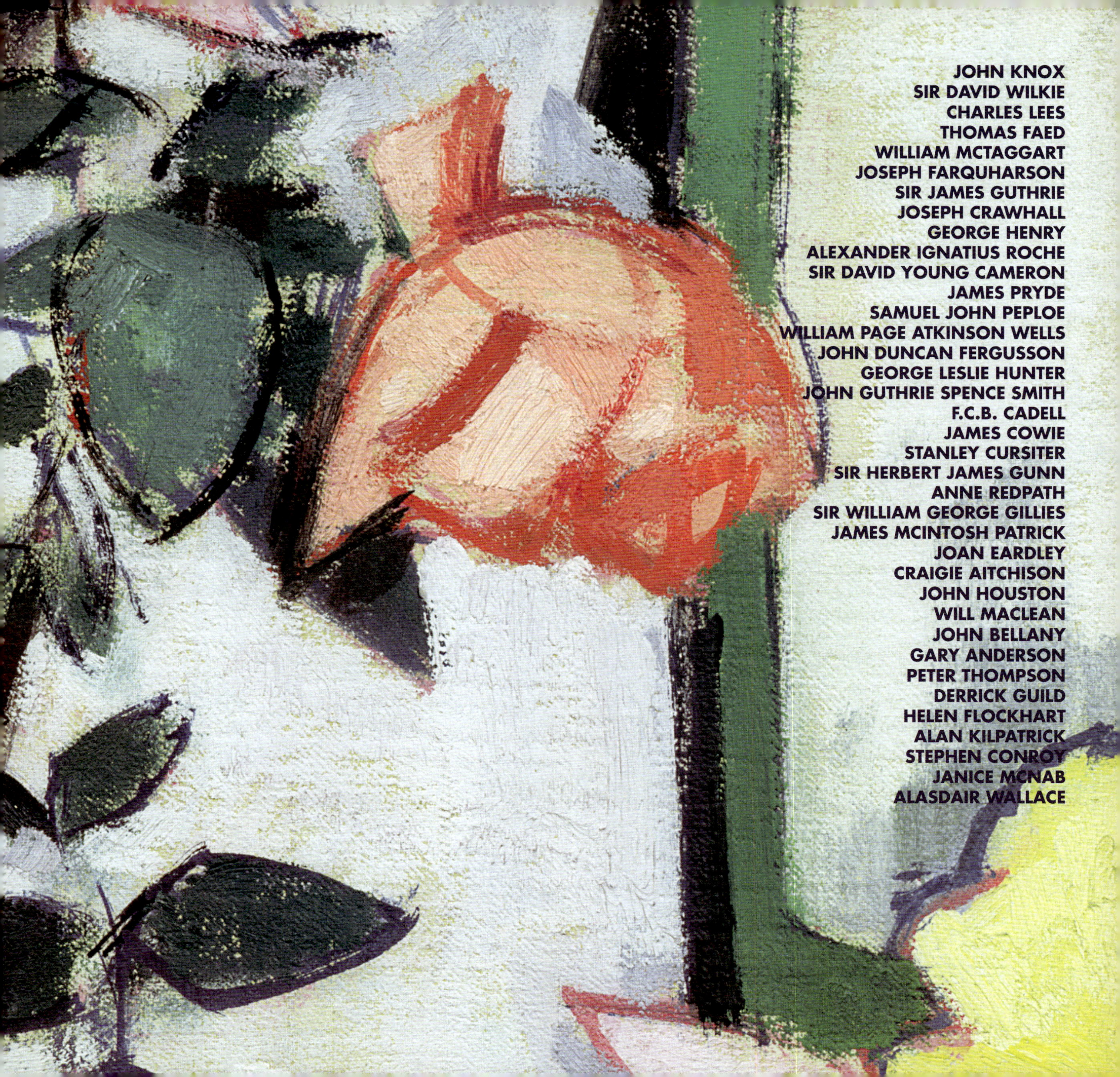

JOHN KNOX
SIR DAVID WILKIE
CHARLES LEES
THOMAS FAED
WILLIAM MCTAGGART
JOSEPH FARQUHARSON
SIR JAMES GUTHRIE
JOSEPH CRAWHALL
GEORGE HENRY
ALEXANDER IGNATIUS ROCHE
SIR DAVID YOUNG CAMERON
JAMES PRYDE
SAMUEL JOHN PEPLOE
WILLIAM PAGE ATKINSON WELLS
JOHN DUNCAN FERGUSSON
GEORGE LESLIE HUNTER
JOHN GUTHRIE SPENCE SMITH
F.C.B. CADELL
JAMES COWIE
STANLEY CURSITER
SIR HERBERT JAMES GUNN
ANNE REDPATH
SIR WILLIAM GEORGE GILLIES
JAMES MCINTOSH PATRICK
JOAN EARDLEY
CRAIGIE AITCHISON
JOHN HOUSTON
WILL MACLEAN
JOHN BELLANY
GARY ANDERSON
PETER THOMPSON
DERRICK GUILD
HELEN FLOCKHART
ALAN KILPATRICK
STEPHEN CONROY
JANICE MCNAB
ALASDAIR WALLACE

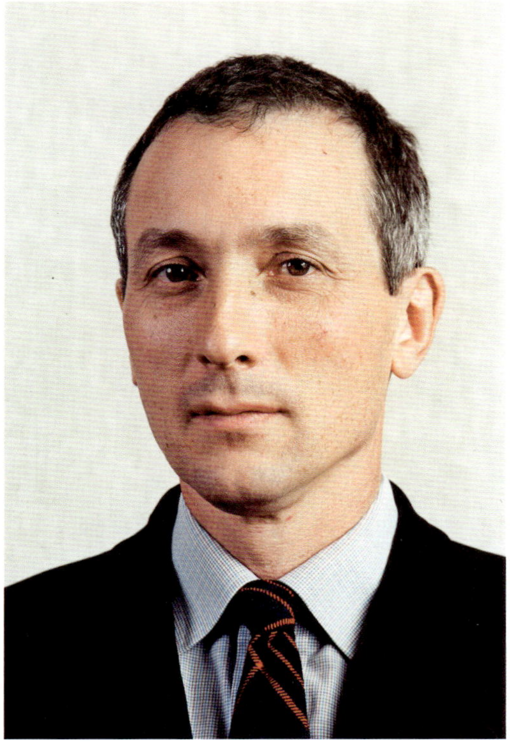

James Holloway trained at the Courtauld Institute at London University and has worked at the National Gallery of Scotland and the National Museum of Wales. He is a specialist in Scottish art and edited the National Galleries of Scotland's series of booklets, *Scottish Masters* including volumes on James Tassie, Jacob More, William Aikman and the Norie family. He is currently working on the *Portrait of the Nation* project to transform the presentation and interpretation of Scotland's national portrait collection. He is a member of the Collections Advisory Panel of the National Trust for Scotland and serves on the committees of the Hopetoun Preservation Trust and the Paxton House Trust.

VIEW OF THE CLYDE LOOKING TOWARDS DUMBARTON ROCK

JOHN KNOX (1778–1845)

oil on canvas, 91.4x147.2 cm

Purchased 1984

'The view of the Clyde and the Vale of Leven from Dalnottar Hill is one of Scotland's finest. John Knox paints in a beguiling image of that Garden of Eden before paradise was lost in the Industrial Revolution. There are hints of change to come: the factory in the middle distance, the tiny steam boat emerging from the east, even the dying light to the west suggest the imminent transformation of peaceful, rural idyll into industrial desolation.

The man responsible for much of that was William Dunn, who by 1835 owned much of the land and many of the mills in the vale. He probably commissioned this painting, possibly to hang in the aptly named Milton House, seen across the first field in the foreground.'

– Chosen by James Holloway, Director, Scottish National Portrait Gallery, Trustee of National Galleries of Scotland.

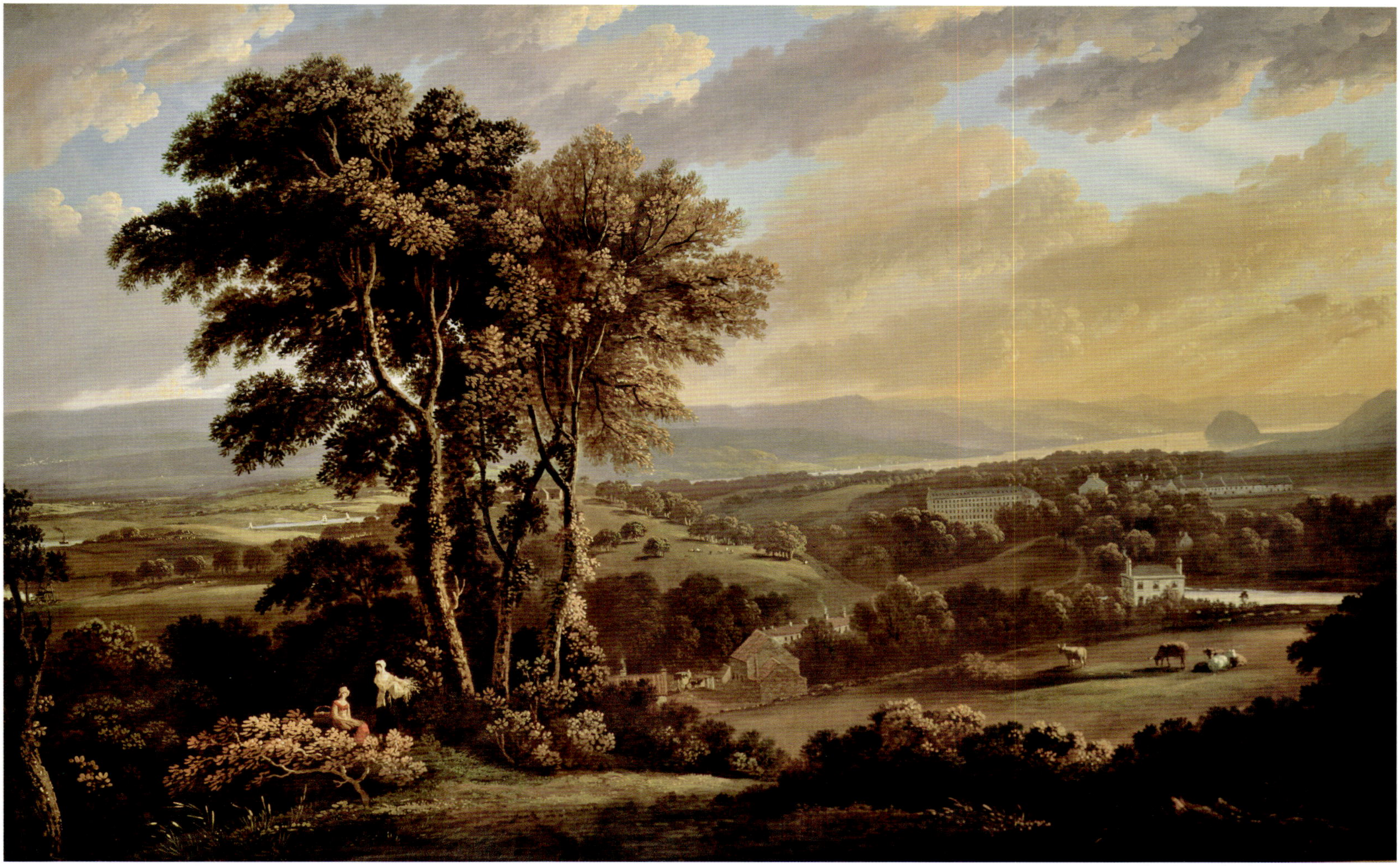

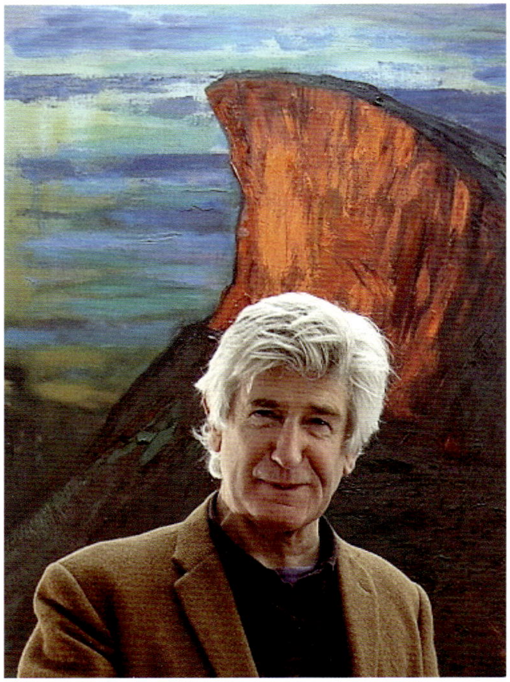

Alexander Moffat studied painting at Edinburgh College of Art alongside his life-long friend, John Bellany. He was Chairman of The New 57 Gallery, Edinburgh (1968–1978) and in 1979 joined the staff of The Glasgow School of Art where he was Head of Painting from 1992 until his retirement in 2005. The Third Eye Centre, Glasgow organised a touring exhibition of his portraits of Scottish Poets (1981–1984) and his work is represented in many collections including The Pushkin Museum, Moscow and the Yale Center for British Art. He has written extensively on Scottish art and has curated several important exhibitions of contemporary painting. In 2004 he was elected to the Royal Scottish Academy and was awarded an OBE in 2006.

CHRISTOPHER COLUMBUS AND QUEEN ISABELLA

SIR DAVID WILKIE RA (1785–1841)

1836, pen and watercolour on paper, 15.8x16.5 cm

Purchased 1981

'Whilst in Madrid – convalescing from illness – during the winter of 1827/28 Sir David Wilkie 'discovered' Velázquez long before Manet, Degas and Monet made their trips to the Spanish capital. Did he ever think, as Renoir had after seeing Velázquez's paintings for the first time, that 'you lose all desire to paint. You understand that it's all been said'. Apparently not, because Wilkie was inspired and invigorated by the three hours he spent each day studying Velázquez's paintings.

In his wonderful drawing of Columbus and Queen Isabella he rivals the Spanish master's subtlety of touch and fluency of expression at every turn. Wilkie's ability to swiftly convey an idea in pictorial terms, to imbue the narrative with an understanding of humanity that could truly be described as Mozartian, fills me with delight. There was no need to make a finished oil painting afterwards. Everything that needed to be said is already there in the sketch.'

– Chosen by Sandy Moffat OBE RSA, Artist and former Head of Painting at The Glasgow School of Art.

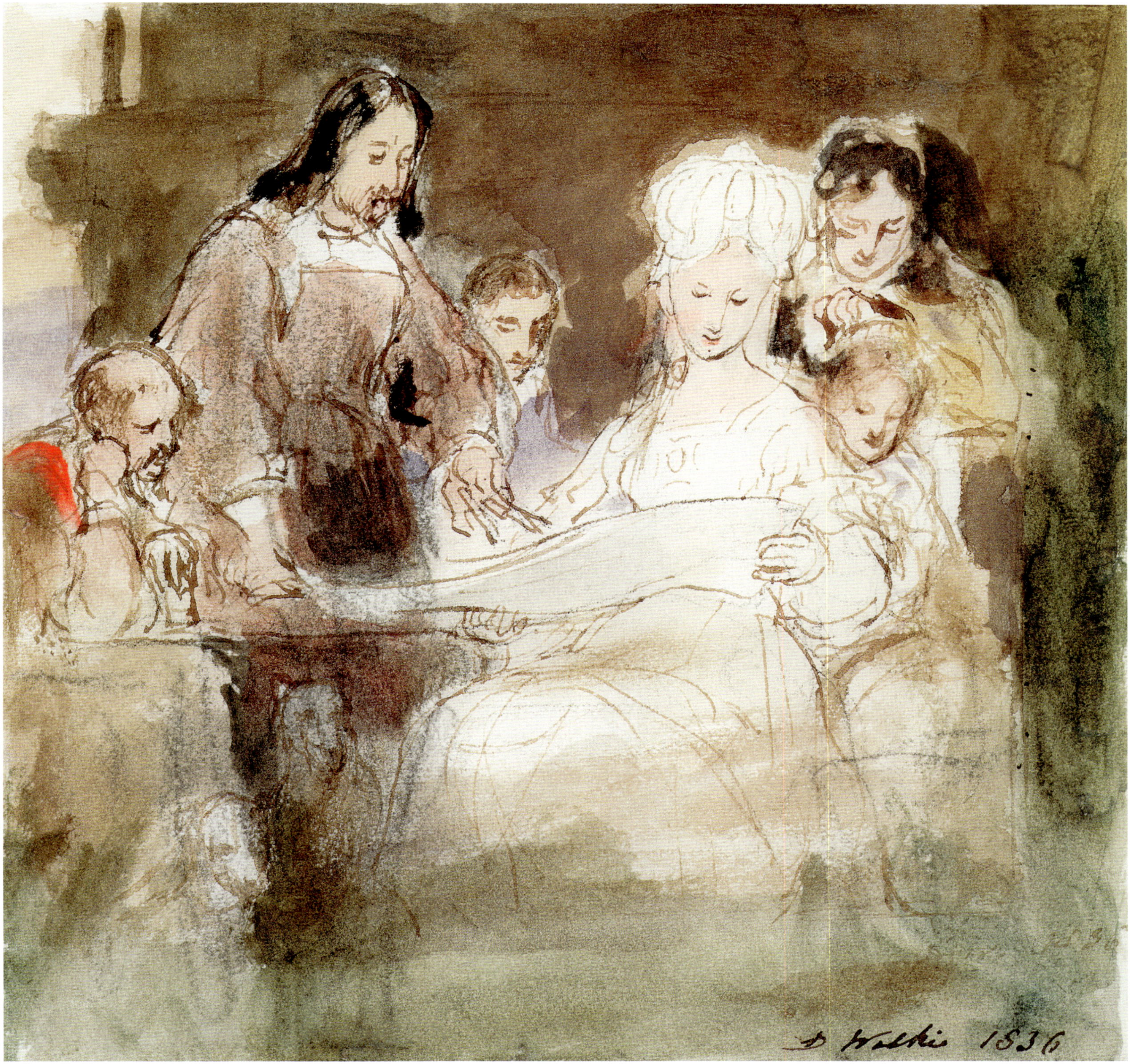
D Wilkie 1836

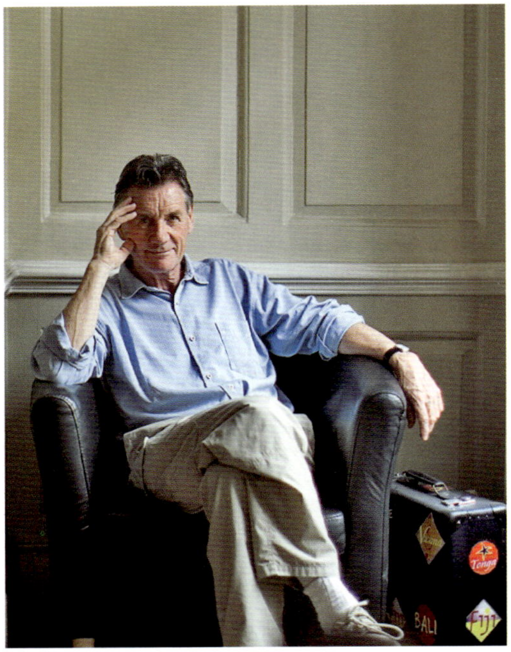

Michael Palin's films include *Monty Python, The Missionary, A Private Function, A Fish Called Wanda, American Friends* and *Fierce Creatures*. Television credits include the plays *East of Ipswich* and *Number 27*, Alan Bleasdale's *GBH* and he has worked on seven BBC1 travel series with accompanying books including *Around the World in 80 Days* and *Hemingway Adventure*. He is the author of the play *The Weekend* and the novel *Hemingway's Chair* and has presented four BBC art documentaries: *Palin on Redpath, The Bright Side of Life* (on the Scottish Colourists), *The Ladies who Loved Matisse* and *The Mystery of Hammershoi*. In 2006 the first volume of his diaries, *1969–1979: The Python Years*, was published, followed by the second in 2009, *1980–1988: Halfway to Hollywood.*

SKATERS: DUDDINGSTON LOCH BY MOONLIGHT

CHARLES LEES RSA (1800–1880)

1857, oil on canvas, 50.8x74.9 cm

Purchased 1980

'An unusual subject, painted with understated skill and delicacy. The movements of the skaters, both fluent and clumsy, have a feeling of celebration and vitality. But what gives the picture a memorable, magical quality, is the play of moonlight on the ice and on the snow-covered banks of the loch. The contrast of the warmth and vigour of the skaters and the bitter chill of the wind blowing through leafless trees, expresses the theme of man against the elements with a light celebratory flourish.'

– Chosen by Michael Palin, Scriptwriter, Comedian, Novelist, Television Presenter, Actor, Playwright.

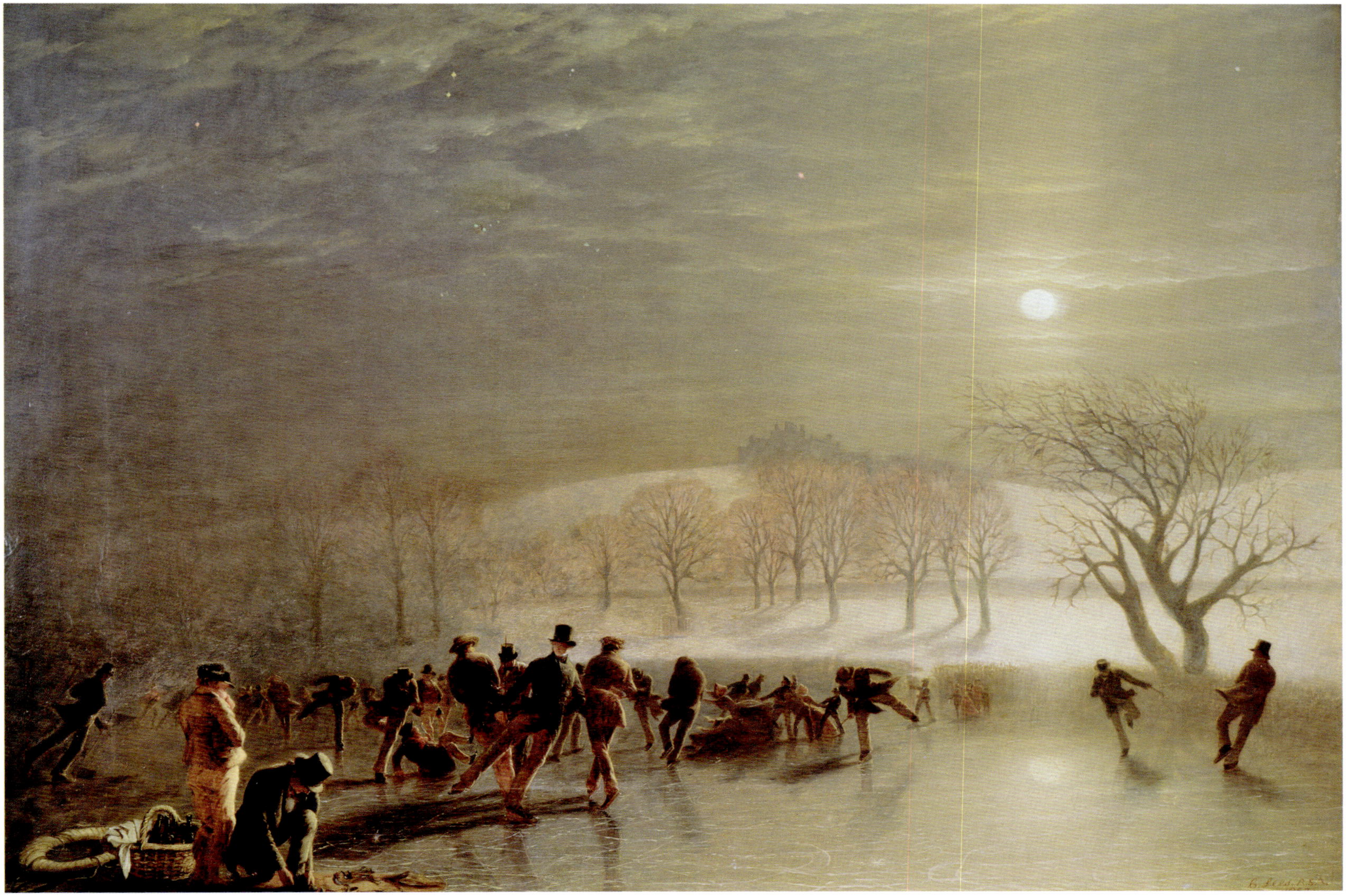

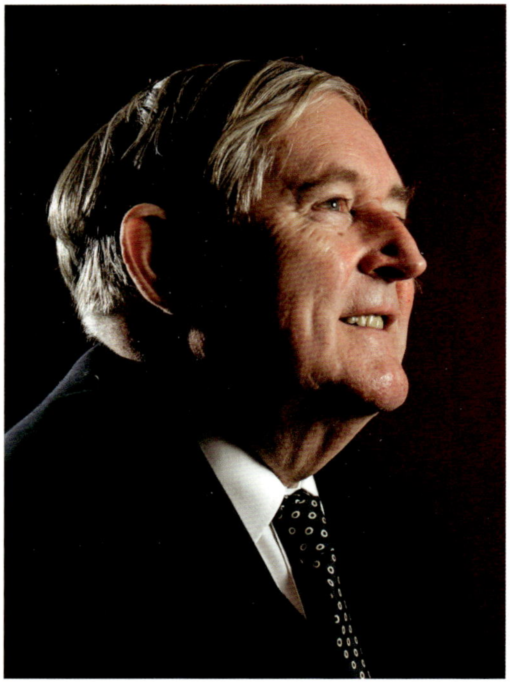

Sir Angus Grossart's principal activity is as Chairman of Noble Grossart Ltd, the Scottish merchant bank he jointly founded. He has served as a director of nearly twenty public companies in the UK and internationally involving banking, investment, investment management, property, drinks, energy, construction, insurance, media, newspapers and other sectors. Formerly he was Vice Chairman of RBS Group and Chairman of Scottish Investment Trust PLC and Edinburgh Fund Managers PLC. Current directorships include Chairman of The Fine Art Society, Edinburgh Partners, Lyon & Turnbull and Scotland International. In the charitable, galleries and museum sectors he is Chairman or Trustee of National Museum of Scotland, Scottish Futures Trust, Culture & Sport Glasgow, Restoration Appeal for The High Kirk of St Giles, Edinburgh, The High Steward of Scotland's Dumfries House Trust; and formerly of the National Galleries of Scotland, National Heritage Memorial Fund and Heritage Lottery Fund in Scotland.

LAST OF THE CLAN

THOMAS FAED RA ARSA (1826–1900)

1865, oil on canvas, 86.3x111.7 cm

Purchased 1968

'This painting arouses close personal thoughts, as well as my appreciation of Faed's fine execution of an evocative scene.

The painting used to hang in Flemings dining room in Crosbie Square. David Donald, who bought it for Flemings, was very encouraging, after Noble Grossart started in 1969. Behind an ascetic exterior, he had imagination and flair, and my occasional visits were always elevated by uplifting talk of paintings and collecting.

This painting also influenced me in the 1980s, to buy for my daughter Flure, the major emigrants painting *The Emigrants – America* by William McTaggart, which had been owned by Reader's Digest in New York, and to repatriate it to Scotland.

We should remember that involuntary emigration was only one side of the story of the Scottish diaspora. What a potent intellectual, mercantile and military influence that diaspora created across the world, reflected not least, in Robert Fleming's move to London.'

– Chosen by Sir Angus Grossart CBE LLD DLitt FRSE DL (MA LLB CA DBA FCIBS Advocate), Chairman of Noble Grossart Ltd, Collector.

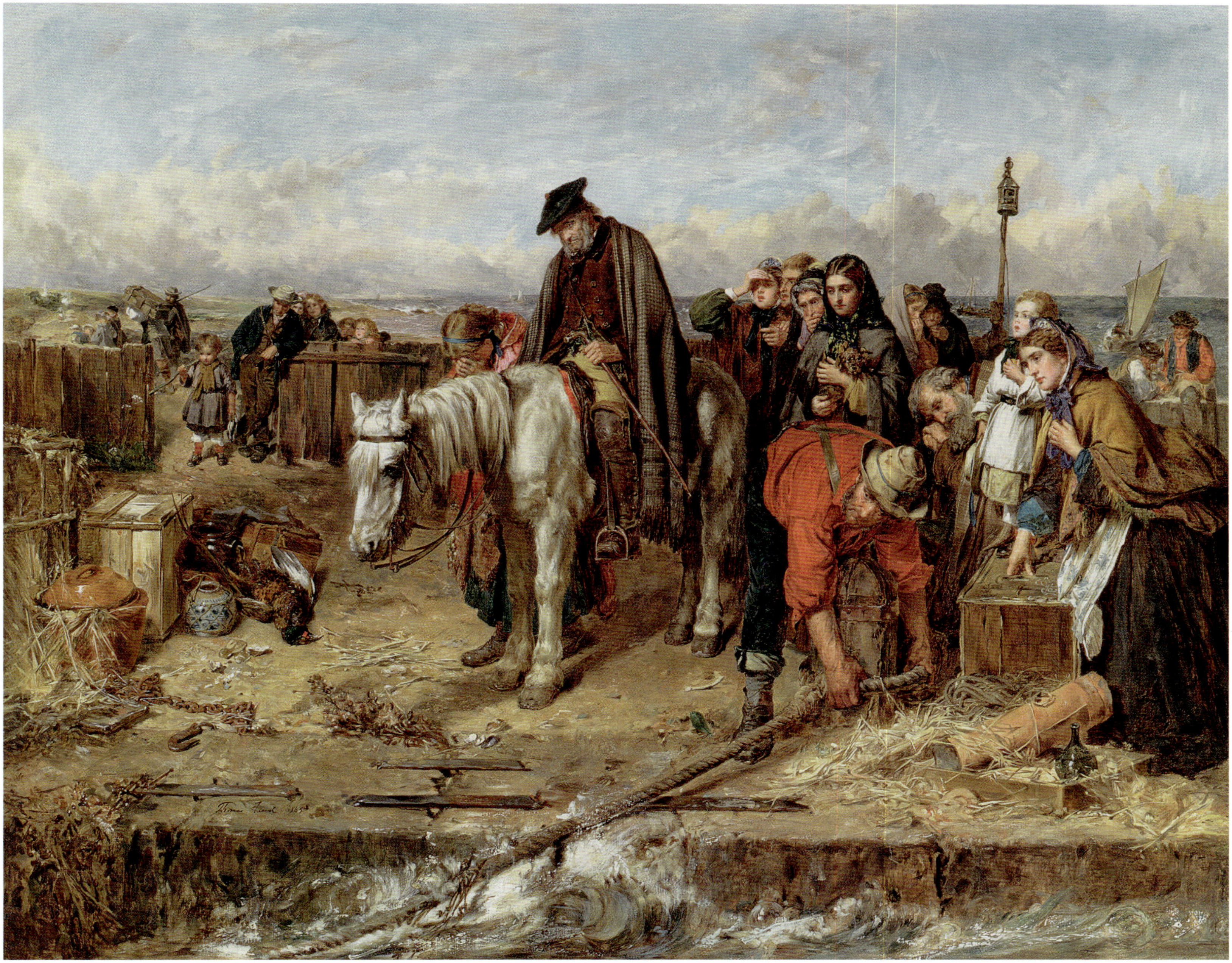

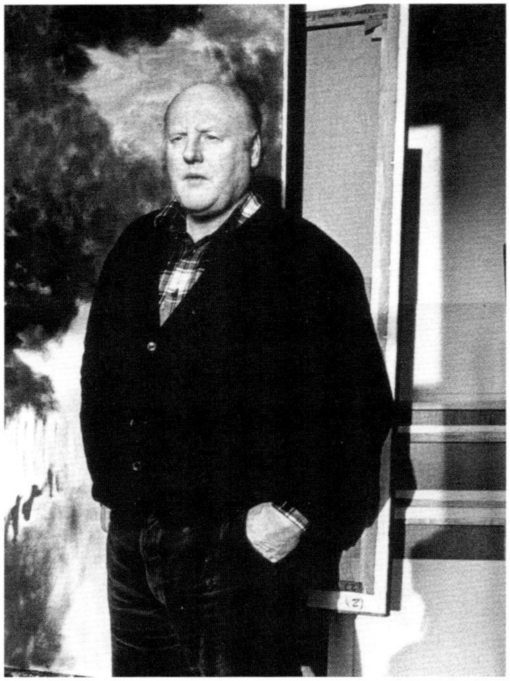

John Houston was born in Buckhaven in Fife and studied at Edinburgh College of Art from 1948 to 1954. He was awarded a travelling scholarship and spent six months in Italy with David Michie 1953–4. Houston joined the teaching staff of the College in 1955 and was Deputy Head of the School of Drawing and Painting from 1982 until his retirement in 1989. He married fellow artist Elizabeth Blackadder in 1956. They travelled widely in Europe, as well as visiting America and Japan. Houston was a confirmed colourist and long admired the work of Turner – a constant companion and hero – and Edvard Munch, and was also inspired by the work of the American artist Mark Rothko and the German painters Emil Nolde, Ernst Ludwig Kirchner and Max Beckmann. A major retrospective of Houston's work was held at the Scottish National Gallery of Modern Art in 2005. Houston sadly passed away months after having selected this work for *Inspired: Forty Years of Collecting Scottish Art.*

THE BARLEY FIELD, SANDY DEAN

WILLIAM McTAGGART RSA VPRSW (1835–1910)

1905, oil on canvas, 99.1x144.8 cm

Purchased 1968

'I've chosen this painting for a few reasons. It reminds me so much of the barley and corn fields in Fife before and during the war when I was young. The light in the painting is so wonderful and also McTaggart doesn't introduce children too obviously, which very often made his paintings a bit sentimental, he didn't need to. To me he was the greatest landscape painter in Britain since Turner. Still very underrated in British art...if only he had been French.'

– Chosen by John Houston OBE RSA RSW RGI, Artist (1930–2008).

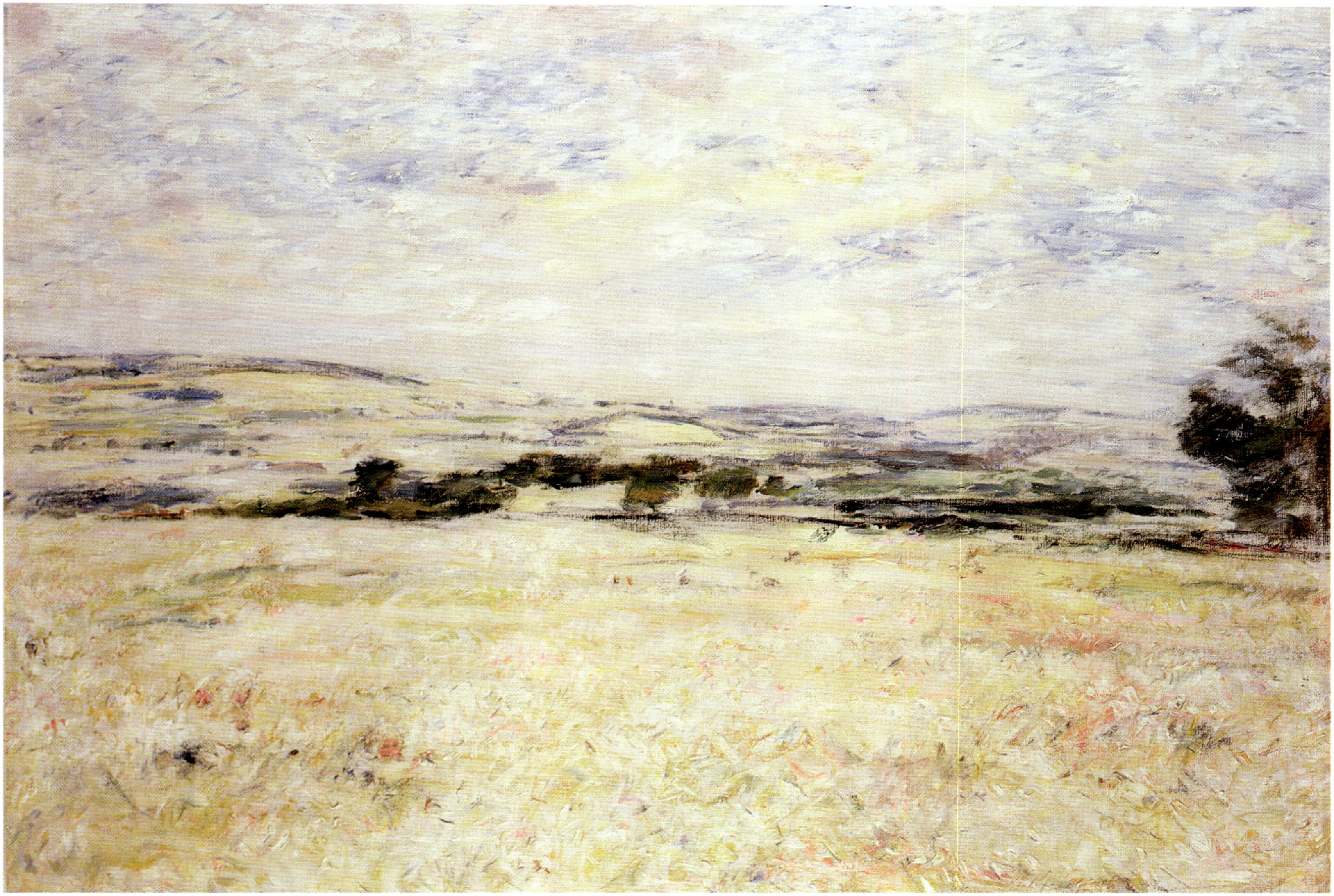

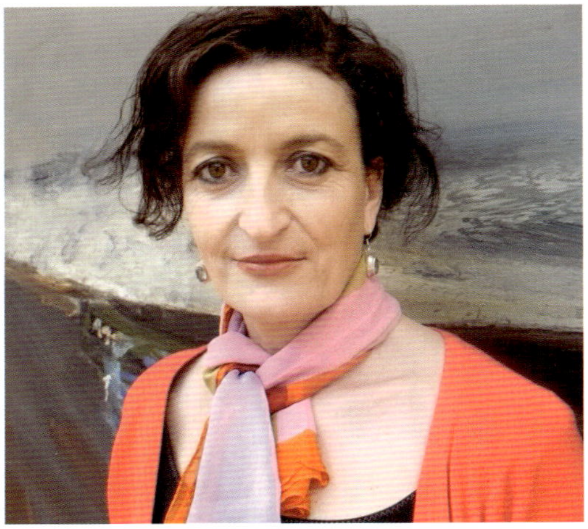

Jennifer Melville has recently been appointed Lead Curator at Aberdeen Art Gallery. She has been Keeper of Fine Art at Aberdeen Art Gallery since 1995. She studied at Aberdeen University and Manchester University and completed a PhD at the University of Edinburgh in 2000. Her research interests are mainly in the area of the late nineteenth-century art and she also actively collects – mainly contemporary art – for the city collections. She is currently Scottish Chair of VAGA and sits on the steering group for Artist Rooms.

FELUCCAS ON THE NILE

JOSEPH FARQUHARSON RA (1846–1935)

c.1885, oil on canvas laid on panel, 16.4x34.9 cm

Purchased 1982

'This fresh and spontaneous sketch is a world away from the paintings for which Joseph Farquharson is best known – snow scenes painted on his estate at Finzean on Royal Deeside. It recalls a period that he spent in Egypt with the famous American artist John Singer Sargent. They had first met in Mürren in Switzerland, when Farquharson tutored the young Sargent and remained good friends. In 1890 Sargent, along with his mother and sister Emily, sailed from Marseille to Egypt. In Cairo, they met up with Farquharson and his stepmother. After a month in Cairo, Sargent and his family, with the Farquharsons, embarked on one of the steamers and went up the Nile to Luxor and Philae. This painting captures perfectly the relaxed atmosphere and pleasures of the upper classes – their leisure lives and delight in foreign travel in a warm country in the middle of a British winter, which is still of course an immense pleasure!'

– Chosen by Jennifer Melville, Lead Curator, Aberdeen Art Gallery.

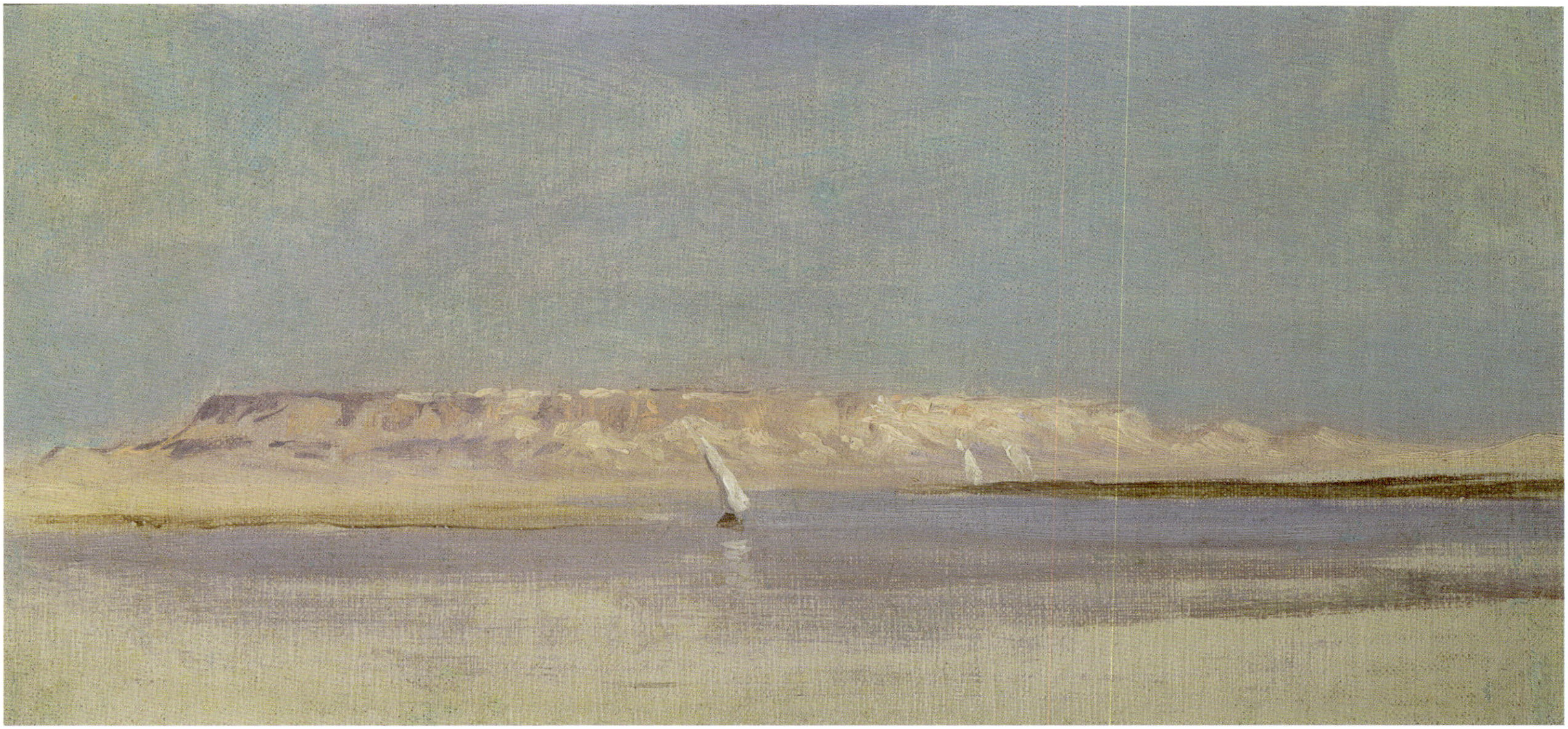

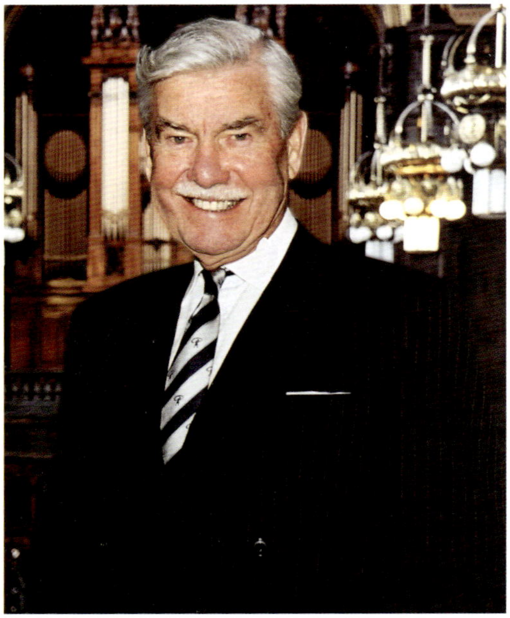

Lord MacFarlane is a lifelong supporter of the arts. He was educated at the High School of Glasgow and was commissioned in the Royal Artillery. In 1949 he founded N.S. Macfarlane & Co. Ltd. which became Macfarlane Group (Clansman) PLC in 1973. He has held a number of important positions in Glasgow and Scotland's business, arts and cultural community including Vice-Chairman of the Scottish Ballet; Director of the Scottish National Orchestra; President of the Royal Glasgow Institute of Fine Arts; Scottish Patron of the National Art Collection Fund and Governor of Glasgow Arts School. Most recently he directed the fund raising campaign for the Kelvingrove Art Gallery refurbishment. Macfarlane was knighted in 1983, elevated to the peerage as Lord Macfarlane of Bearsden in 1991, appointed a Knight of the Thistle in 1996 and received the Freedom of the City of Glasgow in 2007.

THE BRIDGE, CROWLAND

SIR JAMES GUTHRIE (1859–1930)

1882, oil on canvas, 31.7x24.7 cm

Purchased 1996

'There was no appointed leader of the Glasgow Boys but had one been chosen it would almost certainly have been James Guthrie. D.Y. Cameron, one of Guthrie's fellow Glasgow painters described Guthrie after his death as a man of strange and alluring personality, pure of heart, greatly gifted, greatly loved and greatly honoured. No meanness of outlook, no ungenerous thought, no petty jealousy strained his life and he was too big to indulge in vain criticism. The Glasgow Boys were fortunate in having fellow artists with whom they could commiserate when things were going badly, and celebrate with when all was going well. Guthrie's closest friends were E.A Walton, Joseph Crawhall and George Henry.

The Bridge, Crowland, in which the tone of the painting is lighter, marks a new stage in Guthrie's progress, and it also illustrates the close relationships of the Boys; as Crawhall who was the most talented animal painter of the Group painted the small dog for Guthrie. Guthrie, who had in his youth been one of the greatest critics of The Royal Scottish Academy, was appointed President of this illustrious institution in 1902, and became arguably its most distinguished holder of this most important office during his seventeen years as President.'

– Chosen by Lord MacFarlane of Bearsden KT DL, Hon Life President of Diageo.

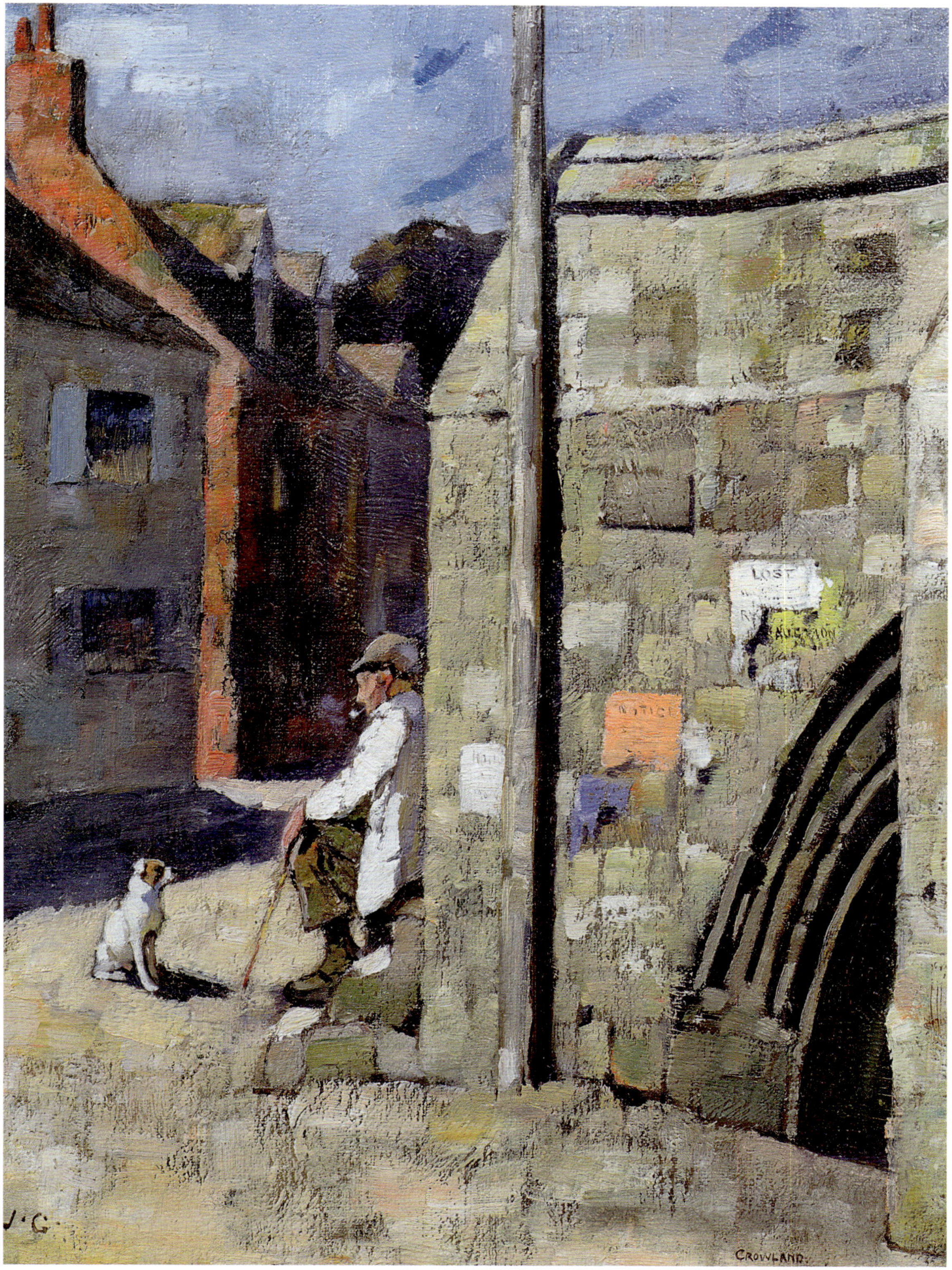
LOST
CROWLAND

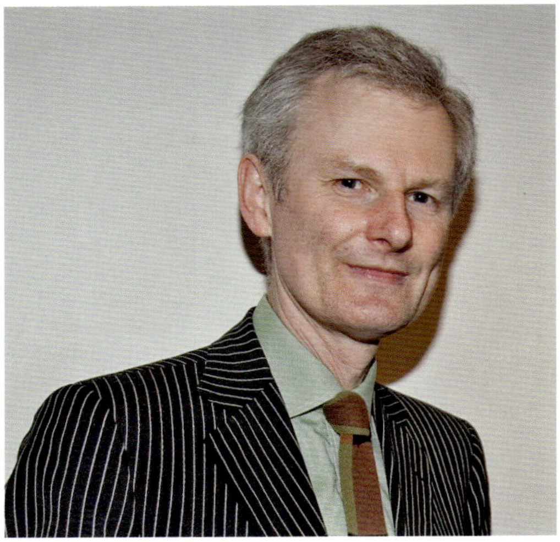

James Knox was appointed to the Board of Trustees of the National Galleries of Scotland in February 2007. He is Managing Director of The Art Newspaper. Prior to this appointment, he ran his own consultancy advising institutional and private patrons on the commissioning of contemporary art. Also a writer and journalist, his books include the biography of pre-war travel writer and aesthete, Robert Byron, and an illustrated survey of the cartoonist and architectural satirist, Osbert Lancaster. He read History of Art at Trinity College, Cambridge and also gained an M.B.A at INSEAD. Born and brought up in Ayrshire, he launched the campaign in 2007 to save Dumfries House and continues to promote regeneration locally through cultural projects. He divides his time between London, Edinburgh and Ayrshire.

THE BULL RING, ALGECIRAS

JOSEPH CRAWHALL RSW (1861–1913)

1891, watercolour on paper, 29.2x42 cm

Purchased 1981

'*The Bull Ring* offers a chance to rediscover Crawhall's star quality. John Lavery wrote that he was "the artist to whom the Glasgow School owed its greatest distinction". In his day, his work excited such competition amongst Glasgow's connoisseur collectors that examples rarely appeared on the open market. Indeed, The Studio reported that: "If you were to offer Mr Burrell a Degas...he would ponder long before deciding to purchase. But if you offered him a Crawhall he would succumb at once." This watercolour reveals why. The sensuality of brushwork and colour combined with a modern's ruthless paring of detail conveys the stillness and danger of the scene. Ironically, Crawhall's desirability – manifest in his glorious watercolours of animals and birds – has caused his relative obscurity today. Out of an oeuvre of around 400 works, 140 alone remain largely unseen in the Burrell Collection. As keepers of flame, the Burrell should act to restore Crawhall to his pedestal of fame.'

– Chosen by James Knox, Managing Director, The Art Newspaper, Trustee of National Galleries of Scotland.

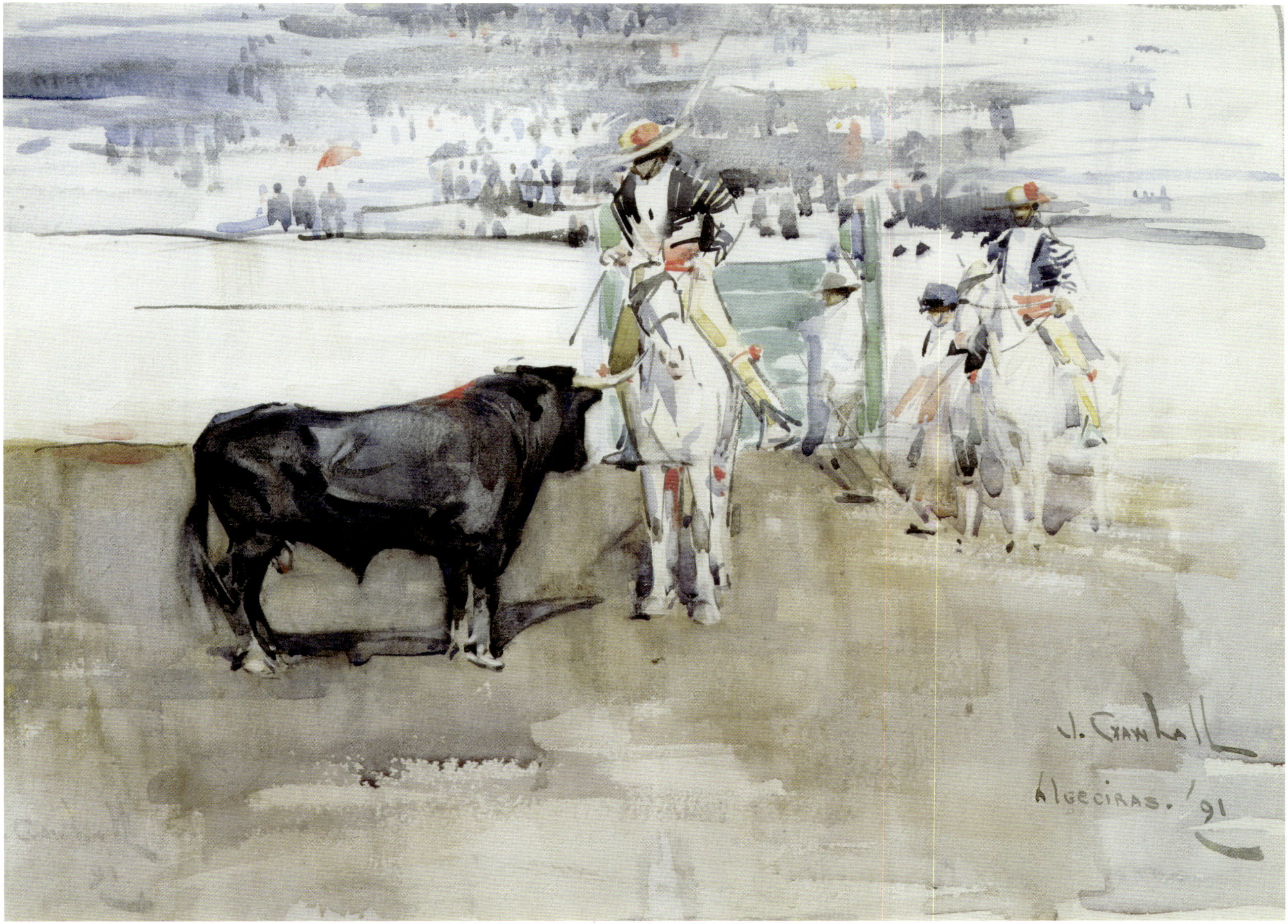
J. Crawhall
ALGECIRAS. '91

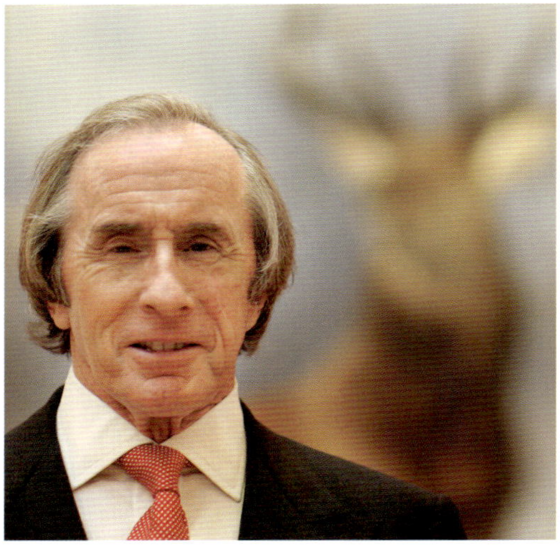

Sir Jackie Stewart's passion for clay pigeon shooting was shared by his grandfather who was a gamekeeper, as well as by his father. He started competitive shooting before he was fifteen and went on to shoot for Scotland and Great Britain. He won the Scottish, Irish, Welsh, English and British Championships, as well as twice winning the Coupe De Nations (European and Mediterranean Championships). In the 1960s he was given an opportunity to compete as a driver by Scottish enthusiast – Barry Filer, and it quickly became clear to others that his skills were such that he could make racing his life. His mother never recognised that he drove but with the support of his bride Helen, the young Stewart rapidly began to dominate British Club racing, and then the British and European Formula 3 scene becoming three times Formula One Motor Racing World Champion. Stewart was knighted in June 2001 and appointed Global Ambassador for Royal Bank of Scotland in 2004.

GIRL READING

GEORGE HENRY RA RSA RSW (1858–1943)

1896, pastel on grey paper, 60.9x69.8 cm

Purchased 1978

'I am a great admirer of Scottish art and have always liked George Henry's work. I think he is a great craftsman. The subtlety of this picture is what first drew me to it; my eye is immediately drawn to the back of her neck. The sketchiness of Henry's lines and simplicity of the composition encourage the viewer to use their imagination rather than providing them all the details.'

– Chosen by Sir Jackie Stewart OBE, Former Formula One Motor Racing Champion, Collector.

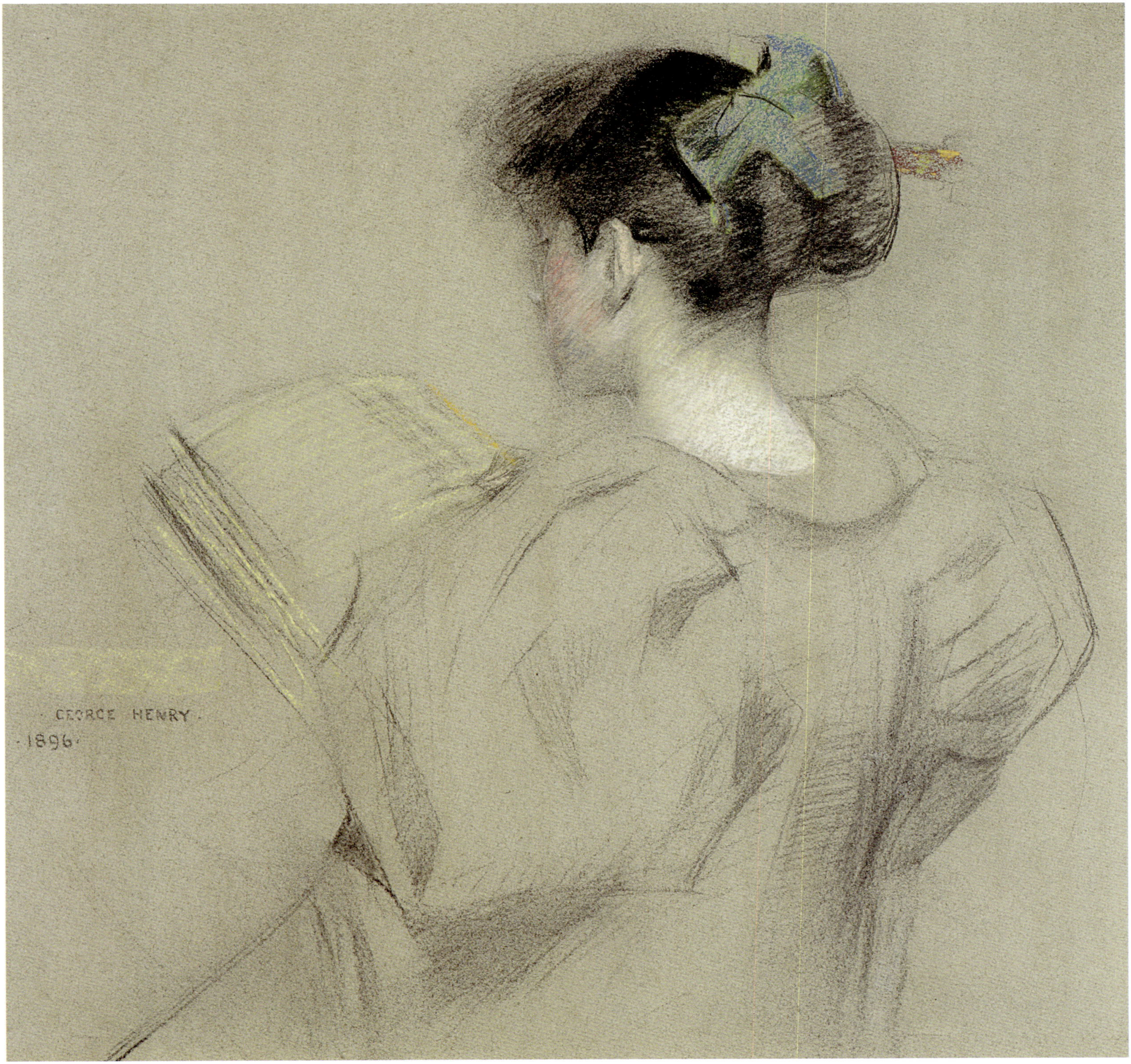
GEORGE HENRY
1896

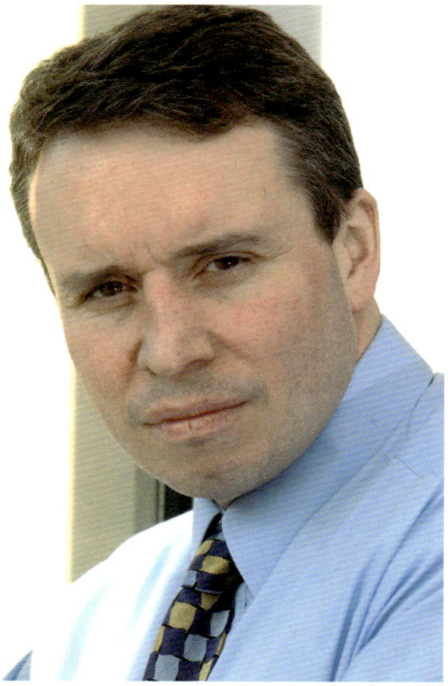

John McLellan was born and raised in Glasgow. In the last twelve years he has edited all three titles at The Scotsman Publications Ltd. Taking the helm at The Edinburgh Evening News in 1997, he moved to Scotland on Sunday, and after a second stint at the News, was named editor of The Scotsman in February 2009. Married with three children, he lives in Edinburgh, and is a keen rugby player, he sits on the Press Complaints Commission, the D-Notice Committee, and is a Trustee of the Radio Forth Cash for Kids appeal.

NEWHAVEN FISHWIFE

ALEXANDER IGNATIUS ROCHE RSA (1861–1921)

oil on canvas, 127x111.8 cm

Purchased 1995

'The fishwife is really a very young girl, already locked into a life of hard labour despite her obvious beauty. This too is the future for the younger girl beside her. The subject has a nervous look – not only is she not used to being the centre of attention but she seems to express a fear for her future. Is the black cat a symbol of fortune that she has a means to make a living, or of bad luck that fate has dealt her and her daughter/sister a hard hand in life?'

– Chosen by John McLellan, Editor, The Scotsman.

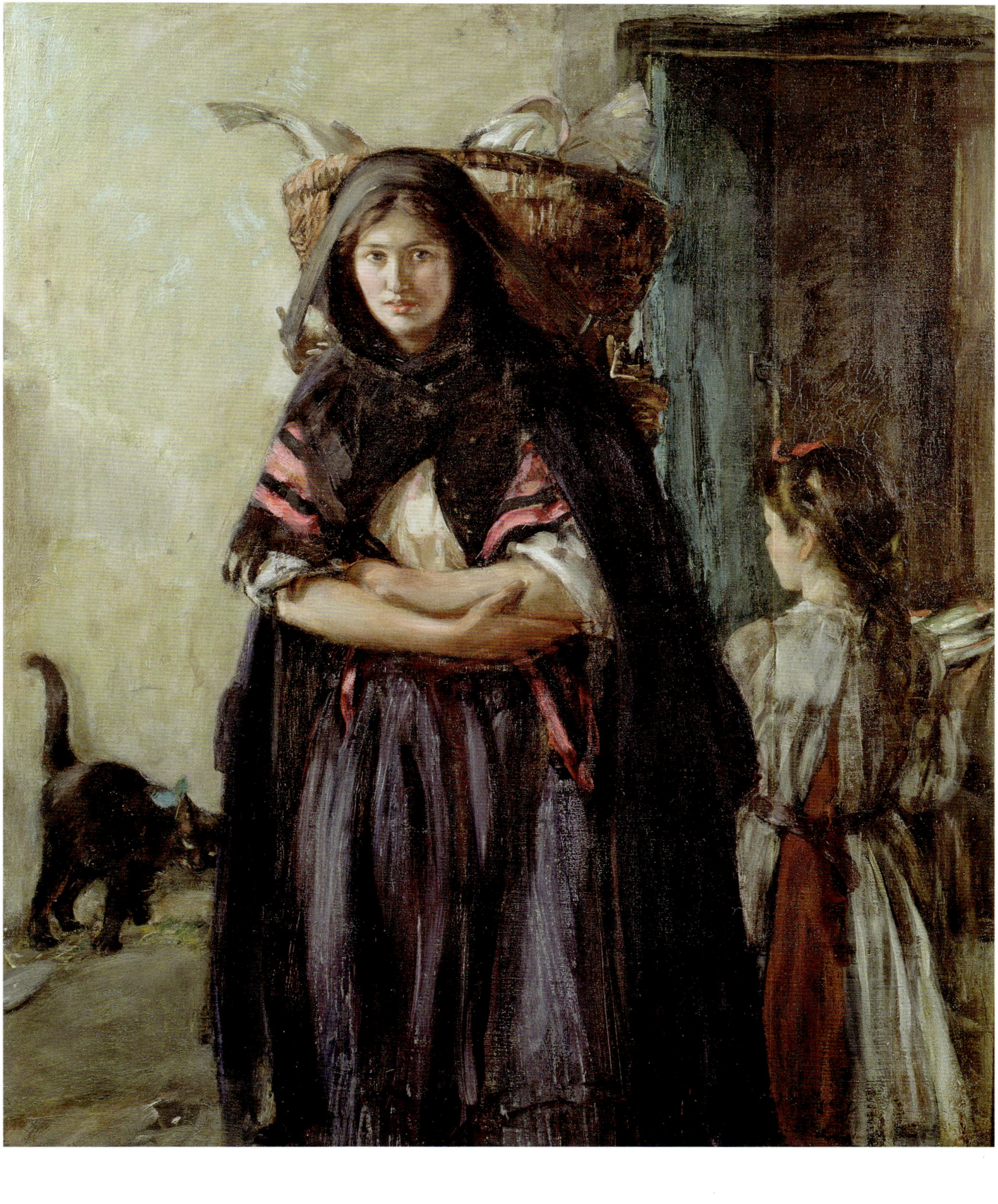

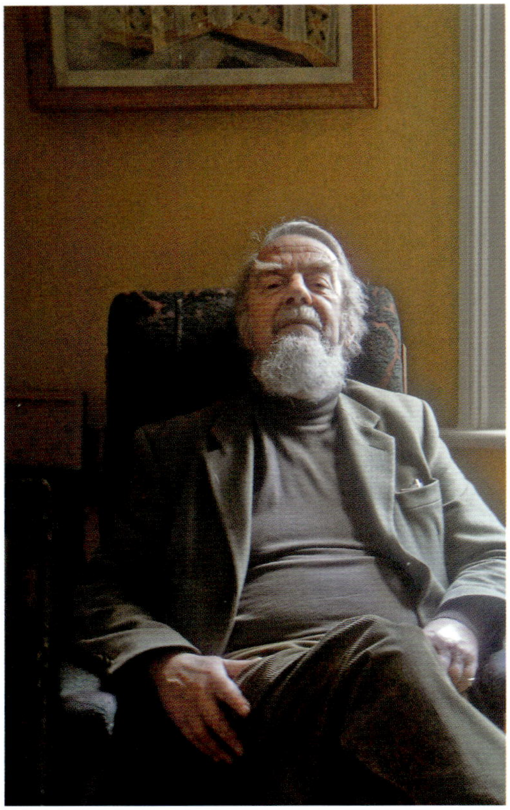

Peyton Skipwith is an independent art consultant, having retired as a director of The Fine Art Society after forty-four years (1961–2005), during which time he organised many exhibitions covering most aspects of British fine and decorative arts of the late-nineteenth and early twentieth centuries, including T*ribute to Edward Bawden, Eric Ravilious in Context* and *Britain Between the Wars*. He is a writer and critic, contributing regularly to various publications including Apollo, The Burlington, Country Life and The Literary Review and is the author of *Joseph Southall 1861–1944, The Great Bird Illustrators and Their Art 1730–1930*, he collaborated with Brian Webb on the Design series of books published by Antique Collectors Club, and with Raymond Booth on *An Artist's Garden*. He is Past Master of The Art Workers Guild.

DIEPPE CASTLE

SIR DAVID YOUNG CAMERON RA RSA RWS RSW (1865–1945)

1896, wash and pencil on paper, 27.9x38.1 cm

Purchased 1992

'There are many treasures to choose from in The Fleming-Wyfold Art Foundation collection, giving one the chance to be self-indulgent. I have chosen this drawing of the Château at Dieppe for several reasons. Not only is it a fine drawing in the great tradition of topographical draughtsmanship stretching back to the eighteenth century, but by the end of the nineteenth century when Cameron made this drawing, Dieppe, thanks to Whistler and Sickert, was becoming the cradle of so much early twentieth-century British art. By a quirk of fate Dieppe is also the city where Gwen John died in 1939. Gwen John, Amaryllis Fleming's aunt, had been Rodin's muse for his *Monument to Whistler*.

Personally, Dieppe remains for me the venue of many happy family holidays, and I recall with pleasure finding and coveting this drawing, but, unable to afford it for myself, earmarking it as a perfect counterpart to the even more romantic Cameron drawing of Holyrood already in The Fleming Collection. Happily David Donald shared my enthusiasm.'

– Chosen by Peyton Skipwith, Writer, Critic, Art Consultant.

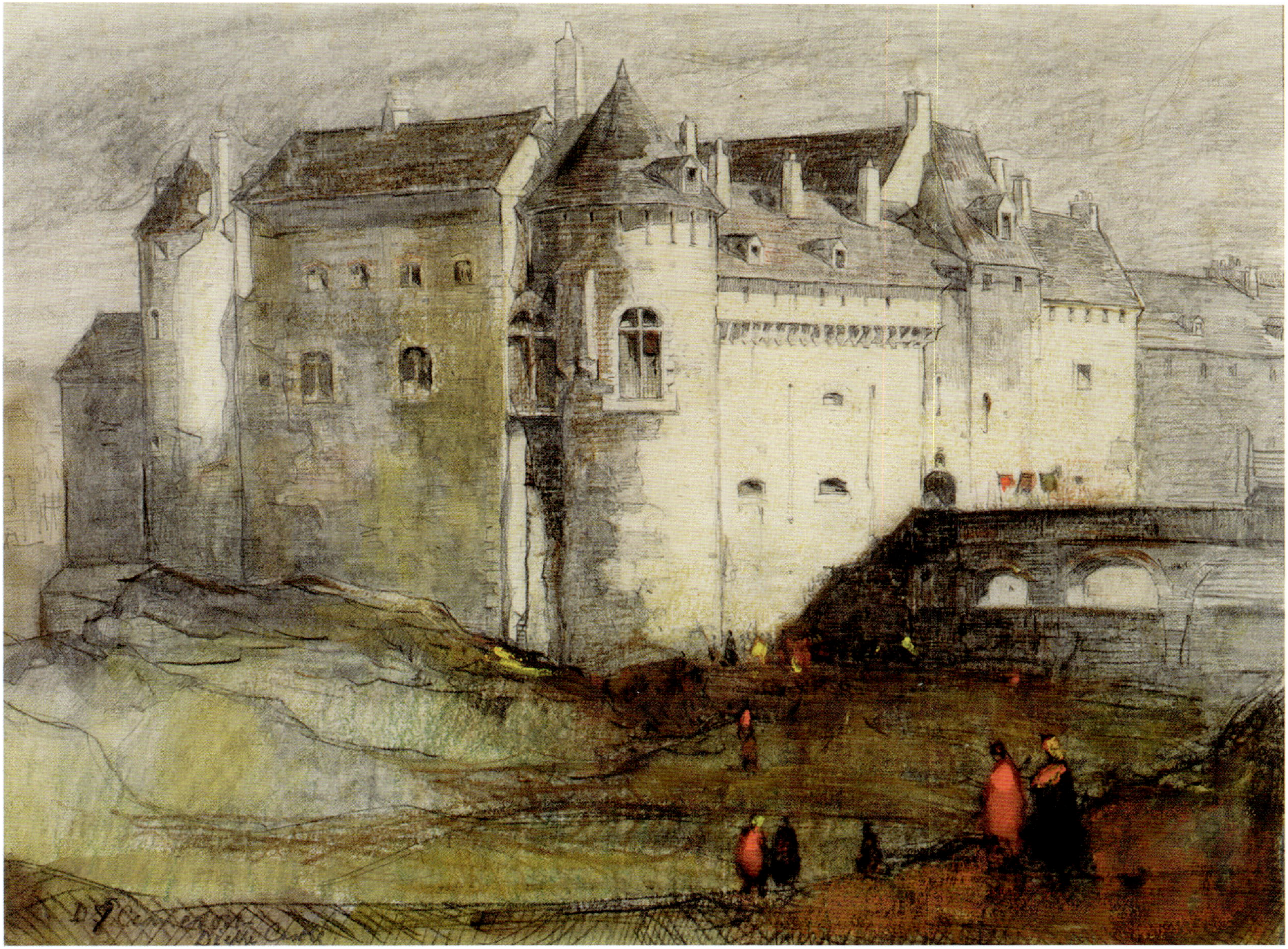

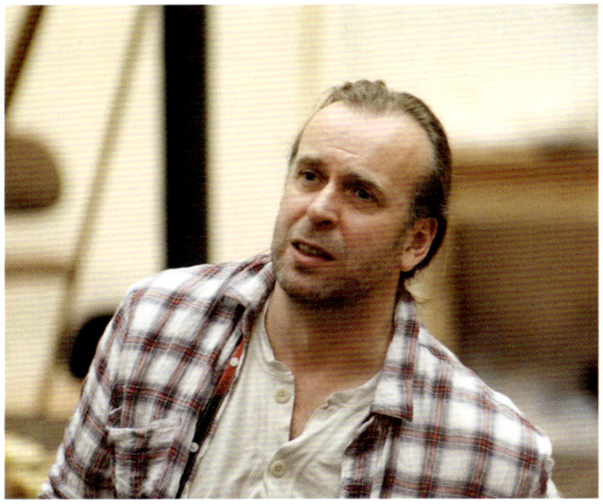

David McVicar recalls that it was as an unhappy Glasgow schoolboy that he became entranced at the age of nine by Ingmar Bergman's film of *The Magic Flute,* which inspired his future career. He became Britain's most precocious opera director, and one of the most sought-after figures in world opera. His first *La Traviata,* directed for Scottish Opera, was a sell-out triumph in 2008. 2009 saw his *Cosi fan Tutte* with Scottish Opera and *Il Trovatore* open at the New York Metropolitan Opera.

THE UNKNOWN CORNER

JAMES PRYDE (1866–1941)

1912, oil on canvas, 18.3x14.9 cm

Purchased 1988

'If it does represent Venice, it's a romantic distillation of that place, reduced to its bare essentials. *The Unknown Corner* is really a stage set for an unknown piece. It's strongly related to the work of Gordon Craig, but also Adolphe Appia and Böklin – the lighting is by Wieland Wagner! It's a painting that cries out to be realised in plastic form – don't be surprised if I pinch its imagery for a show one day.'

– Chosen by David McVicar, Opera Director.

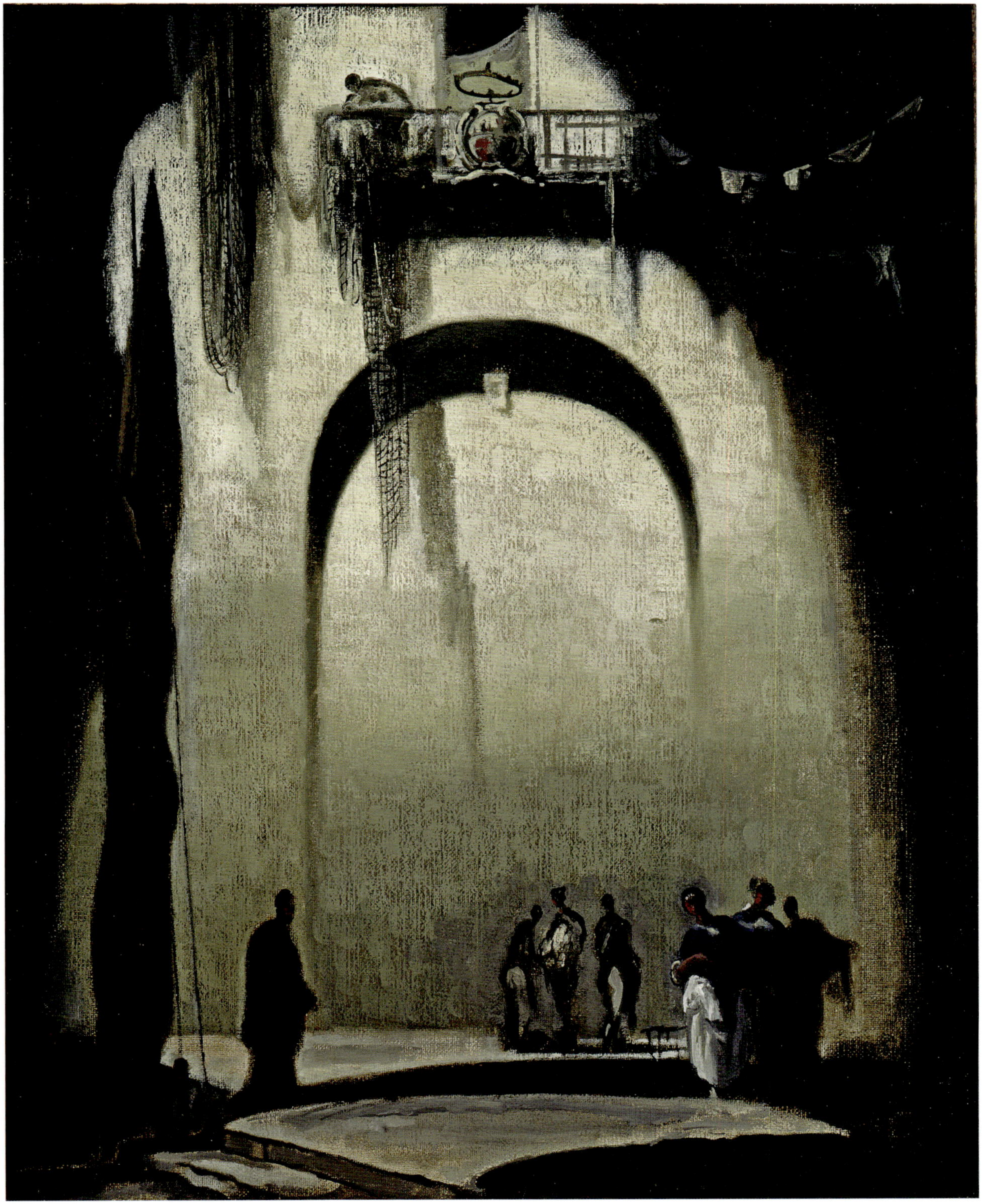

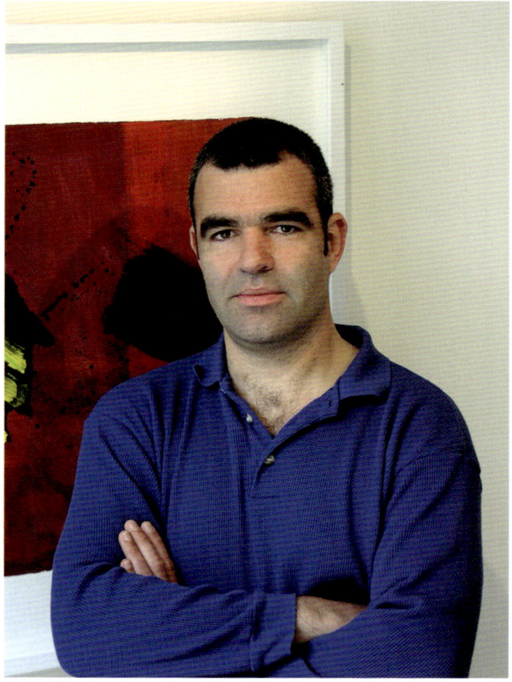

Guy Peploe has written widely on the Scottish Colourists, twentieth century and contemporary Scottish art. Broadcasts include *The Bright Side of Life* (on the Scottish Colourists), a documentary with Michael Palin. He studied French at the University of Grenoble and History of Art at the University of Aberdeen. He has worked at The Scottish Gallery, Edinburgh since 1983 becoming Managing Director in 1992.

LADY IN A WHITE DRESS

SAMUEL JOHN PEPLOE RSA (1871–1935)

1906, oil on panel, 30.4x35.5 cm

Purchased 1968

'Peploe's figure paintings were very important to him: he needed an inspirational connection to the model, but also set himself difficult formal issues to overcome: expression, pose and setting. *Lady in White* is a perfect, small example of this in his exacting, exciting, early *alla prima* technique.'

– Chosen by Guy Peploe, Grandson of the Artist.

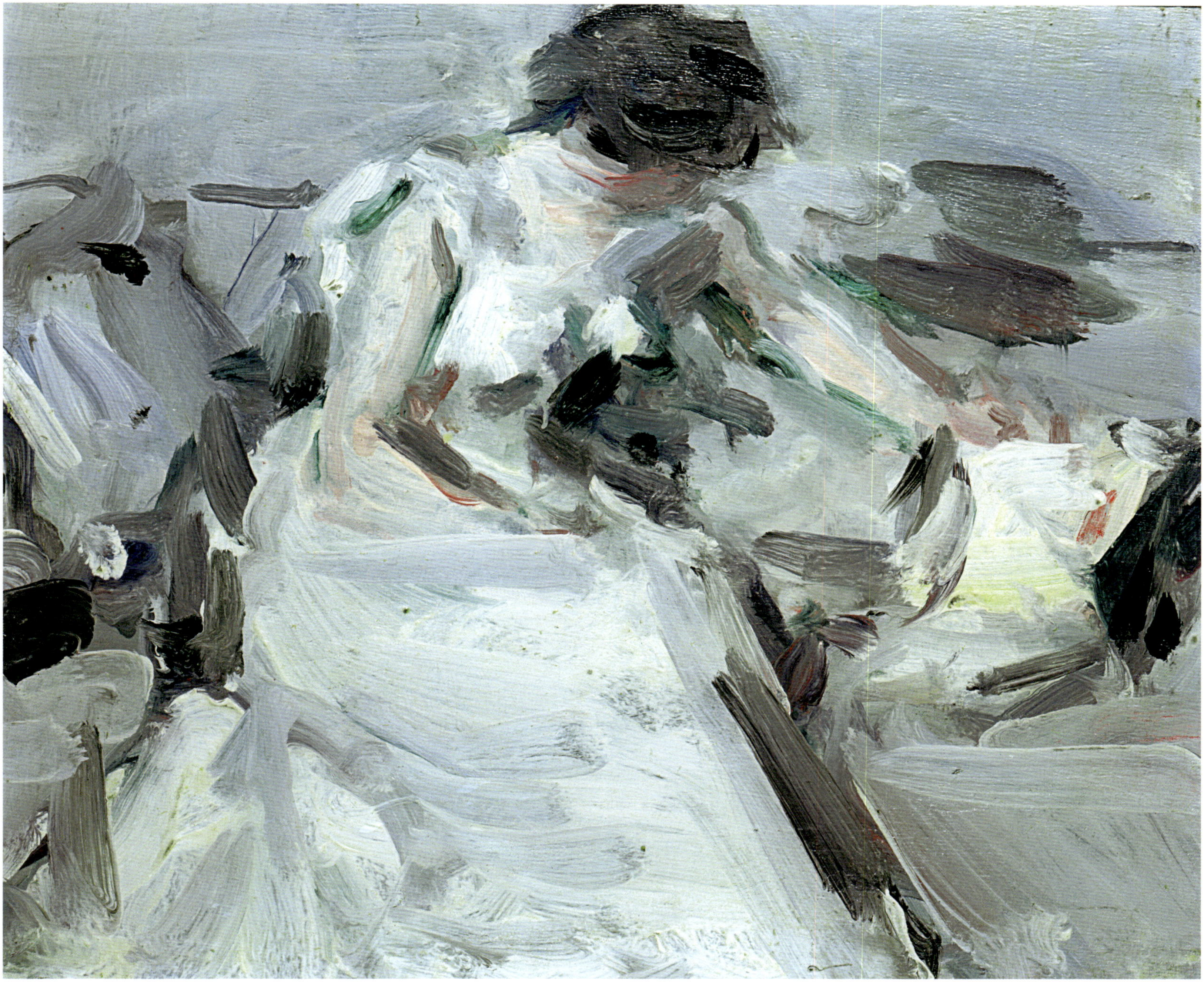

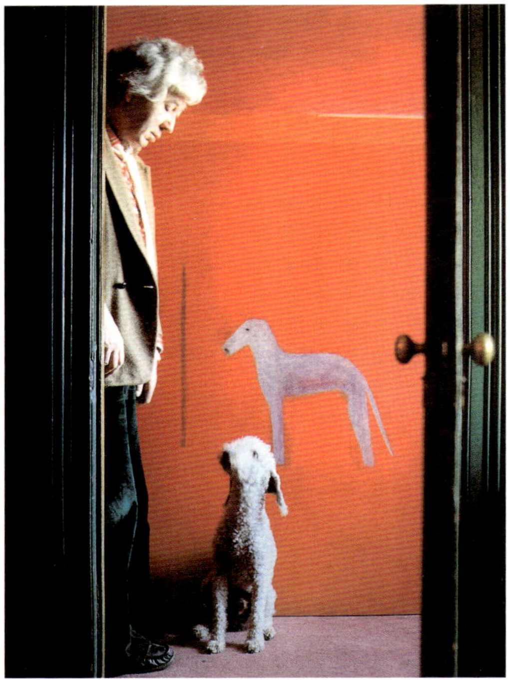

Craigie Aitchison was born in Edinburgh and like his father Lord Aitchison (the first socialist politician to hold the post of Lord Advocate for Scotland) he studied Jurisprudence, enrolling at the University of Edinburgh in 1944 and Middle Temple City of London in 1948. He enrolled as a part-time student at Slade School of Art in 1952 and won the annual prize for best still life in 1953, a subject he explored throughout his career. Other characteristic subjects are the Crucifixion, Italian and Scottish landscape painting and portraiture. The subject of many solo shows, major shows included the Arts Council of Great Britain retrospective exhibition at the Serpentine in London, 1981–2; the Gallery of Modern Art Glasgow in 1996; and the Royal Academy of Arts, London in 2003. Elected a Royal Academician in 1988, he won the inaugural Jerwood Prize for painting in 1994, and in 1999 was awarded a CBE for his contribution to British art. Aitchison died in December 2009.

FEEDING THE HENS

WILLIAM PAGE ATKINSON WELLS RBA (1872–1923)

oil on canvas, 50x40 cm

Purchased 1981

This painting was chosen by Craigie Aitchison when Lucia Lindsay visited him at his south London home in 2009.

Like Aitchison, Wells was born in Scotland and attended the Slade School of Art in London. In keeping with The Glasgow Boys, Wells's interest in the Barbizon School and the time he spent in Paris, led him to favour rustic subject matter painted in earthy tones. Aitchison was drawn to the simplicity of this composition and the delicate handling of colour tones.

Both artists have highly personalised styles, while Aitchison uses oil sparingly, Wells gives the paint surface a three dimensional effect by building up generous layers of paint applied with small brush strokes. The resulting canvases are imbued with a rare sensuality of tone arresting the viewer in a moment of inward reflection.

– Chosen by Craigie Aitchison CBE RA, Artist (1926–2009).

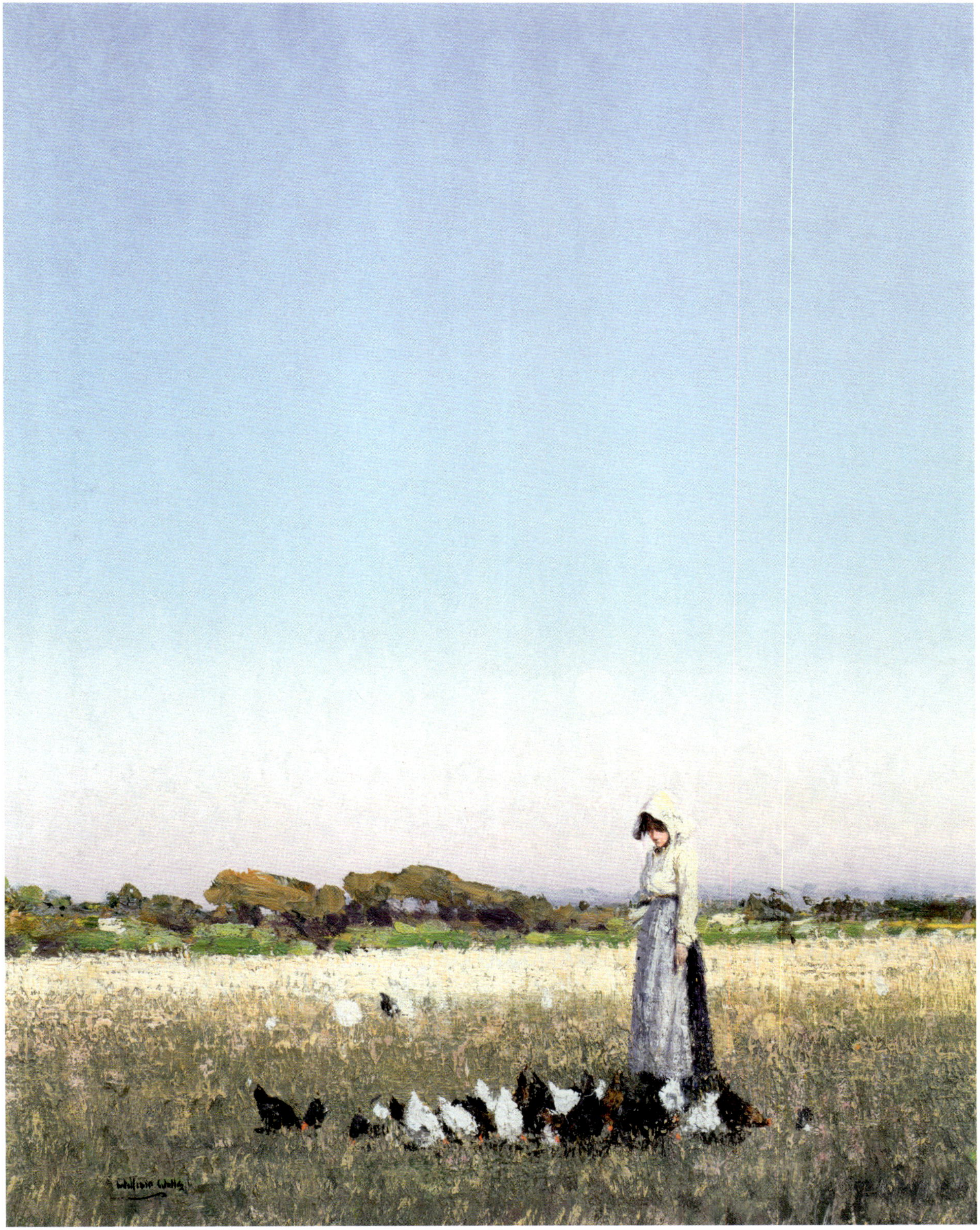

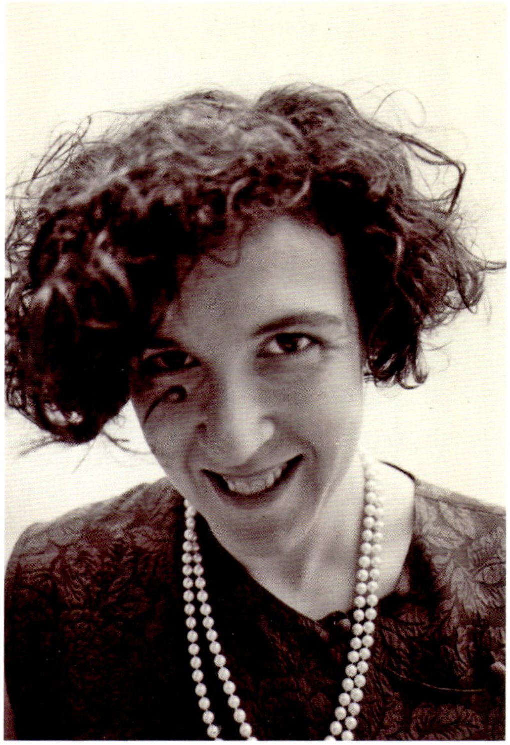

Jackie Wullschlager was born in London and educated at Oxford University. She is the Chief Art Critic of the Financial Times, where she has worked since 1986. Her books include *Chagall: Love and Exile, Hans Christian Andersen: The Life of a Storyteller* and *Inventing Wonderland: The Lives and Fantasies of Lewis Carroll, Edward Lear, J.M. Barrie, Kenneth Grahame and A.A. Milne.*

JONQUILS AND SILVER

JOHN DUNCAN FERGUSSON RBA (1874-1961)

1905, oil on canvas, 50.8x45.7 cm

Purchased 1971

'"A painter can say all he wants to with fruit and flowers", Manet once said. The delicate, subdued palette of pink and silver makes John Duncan Fergusson's early masterpiece *Jonquils and Silver* a far from typical Scottish Colourist work, yet it is a marvellous example of his engagement with French painting, especially Manet, in the first years of the twentieth century. The voluptuous flowers against an enveloping velvety black ground, set off by the thickly painted linen cloth and the shimmering reflections of the fallen bloom in the silverware, inform a composition of great simplicity and restraint. I love it as a modern vanitas painting, and for the transcendent quality of the light. And everything here heralds Fergusson's characteristic balance of elegant design and tonal subtly with an ebullient expressiveness that announced him from the start as the most engaging and ambitious of the Colourists.'

– Chosen by Jackie Wullschlager, Chief Art Critic, Financial Times.

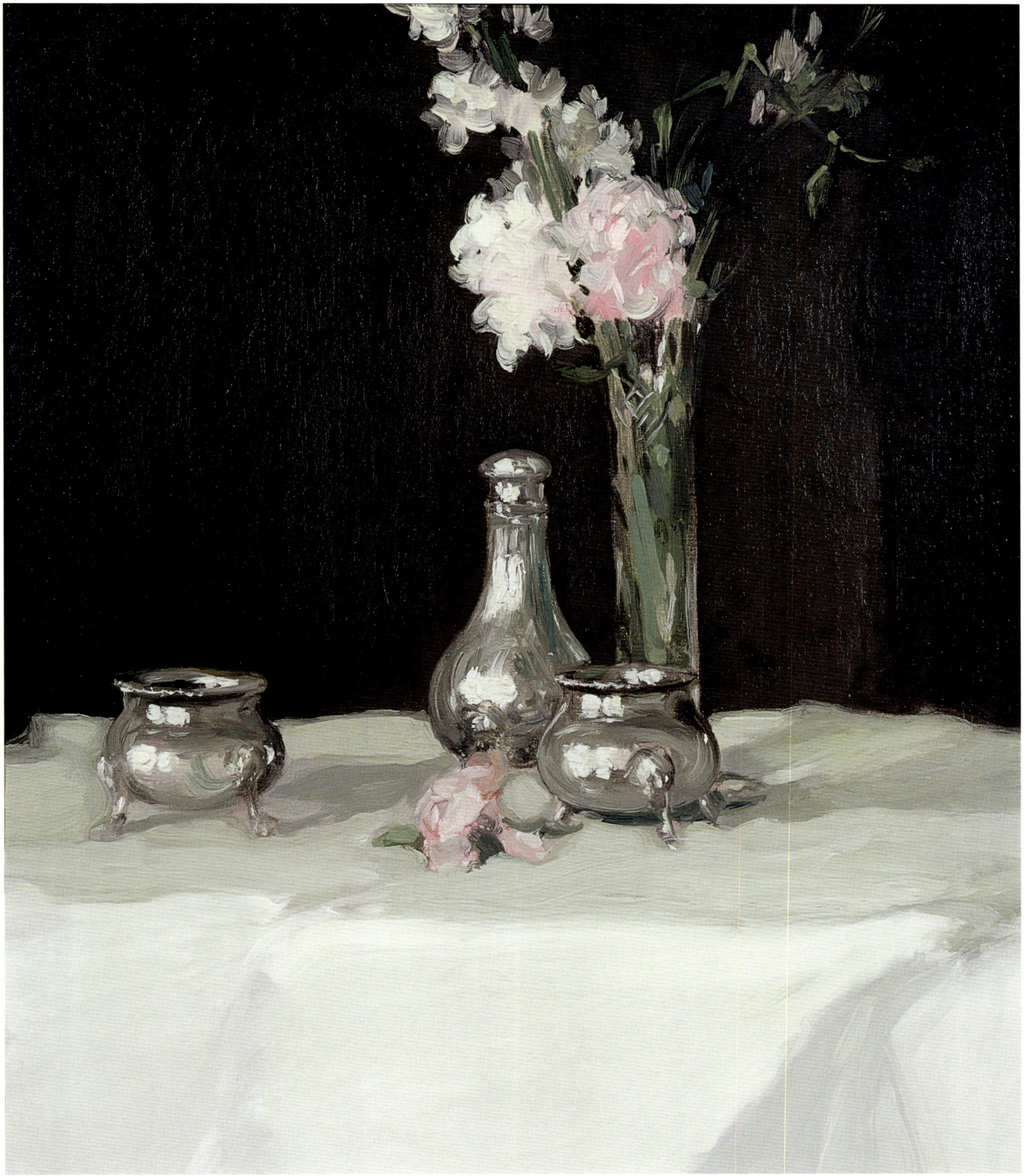

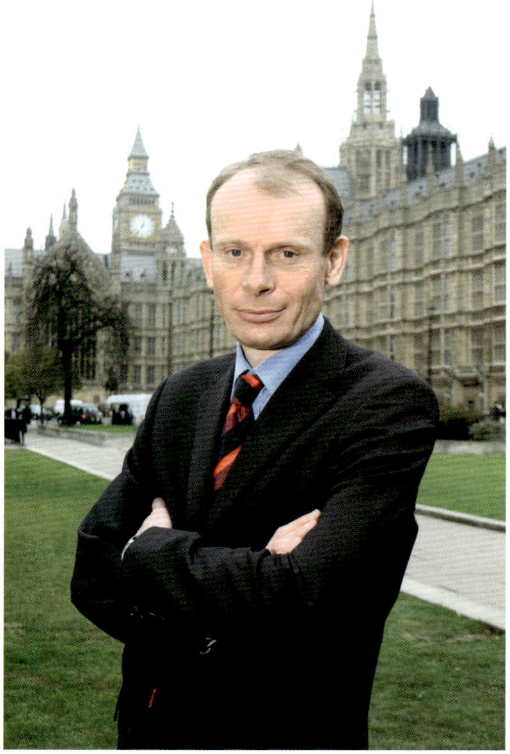

Andrew Marr was born and educated in Scotland and studied English as an undergraduate in English at Trinity College, Cambridge. He began his career at The Scotsman as a trainee and junior business reporter in 1981, he was part of the launch staff of The Independent and worked as Columnist and Political Editor at the Economist before returning to The Independent. He became the BBC Political Correspondent in 2000 and today hosts *The Andrew Marr Show* on Sundays and BBC Radio 4 *Start the Week*.

PEONIES IN A CHINESE VASE

GEORGE LESLIE HUNTER (1877–1931)

c.1928, oil on board, 61x50.8 cm

Purchased 1968

'Hunter was my great or maybe my great-great uncle, but it isn't because of that, I hope, that he's my favourite of the Colourists. His brushwork, a kind of dryish scrumbling very obvious here and in his great pictures of houseboats, is all his own, though his debt to the Matisse of the 1920s is obvious. His best work is better than that of any other interwar slot; his worst is very bad. The "ill health" often mentioned is a euphemism: he drank himself to death. But – salut!'

– Chosen by Andrew Marr, Journalist.

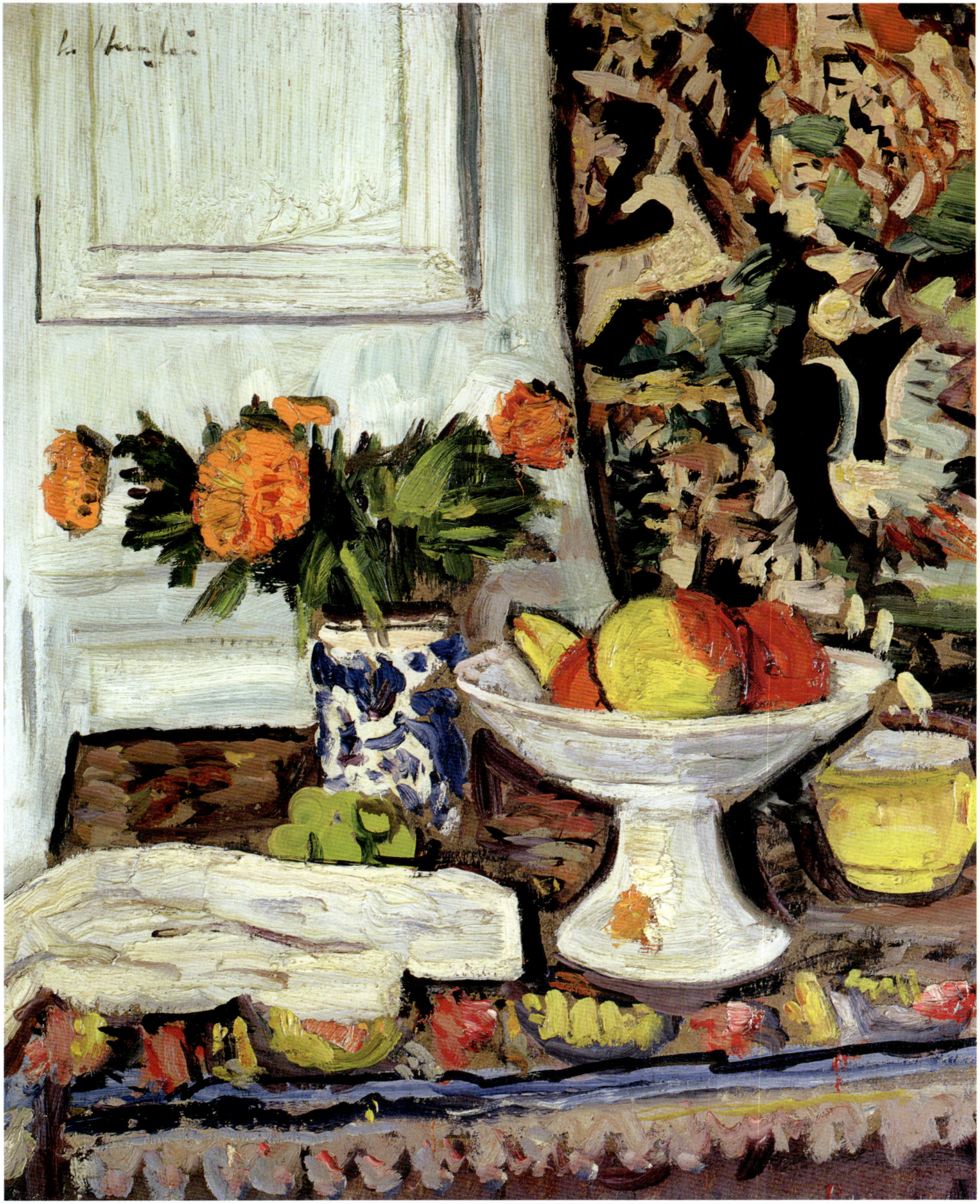

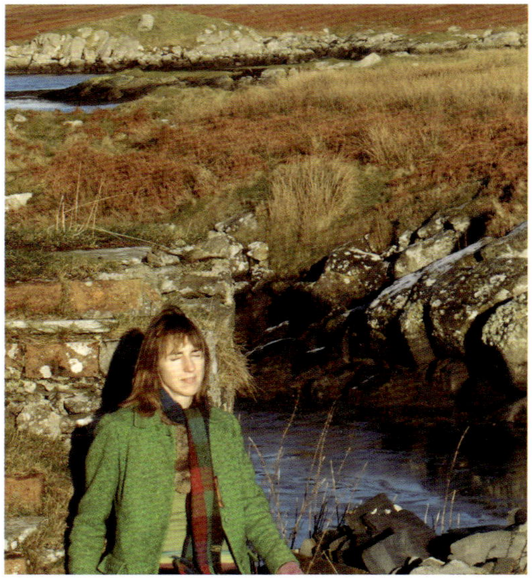

Mary Miers is an architectural historian and journalist and has also worked in the field of historic building conservation. In the 1980s she set up and ran Scotland's Buildings at Risk Register. She is the author of *The Western Seaboard* and *Highland and Islands of Scotland (Poetry of Place)* and co-author of Scotland's *Endangered Houses*. Her family home is in South Uist.

BALLACHULISH QUARRIES

JOHN GUTHRIE SPENCE SMITH RSA (1880–1951)

oil on canvas, 87.6x100.3 cm

Purchased 1980

'One of the things I find fascinating about the West Highlands is the way the landscape, so widely celebrated for its untamed beauty and sublime grandeur, bears the impress of rural industry, and the great engineering feats of road, canal and railway that opened up the glens.

Smith's powerful painting is both a record of this industrial endeavour and a beautiful, almost decorative, composition. I love the contrast of human scale against the drama of the landscape; the way foreground activity is rendered in detail against the bold, painterly blocks of colour. Sgorr na Ciche – the Pap of Glencoe – towers over one of the vast slate mines at Ballachulish, where quarrying began in the 1690s. The quarries closed in 1955, but when the artist came here in the early twentieth century they were producing twenty-six million slates a year – the thick, blueish grey slate of Ballachulish that has become synonymous with the Highland vernacular. "...long neat rows of slate-covered cottages...the crowd, the activity, noise, and bustling industry of this place, contrast agreeably with the stillness, solitude and silence of the scene behind" wrote William Larkin on visiting Ballachulish in 1818.'

– Chosen by Mary Miers, Architectural Writer; Art and Books Editor, Country Life.

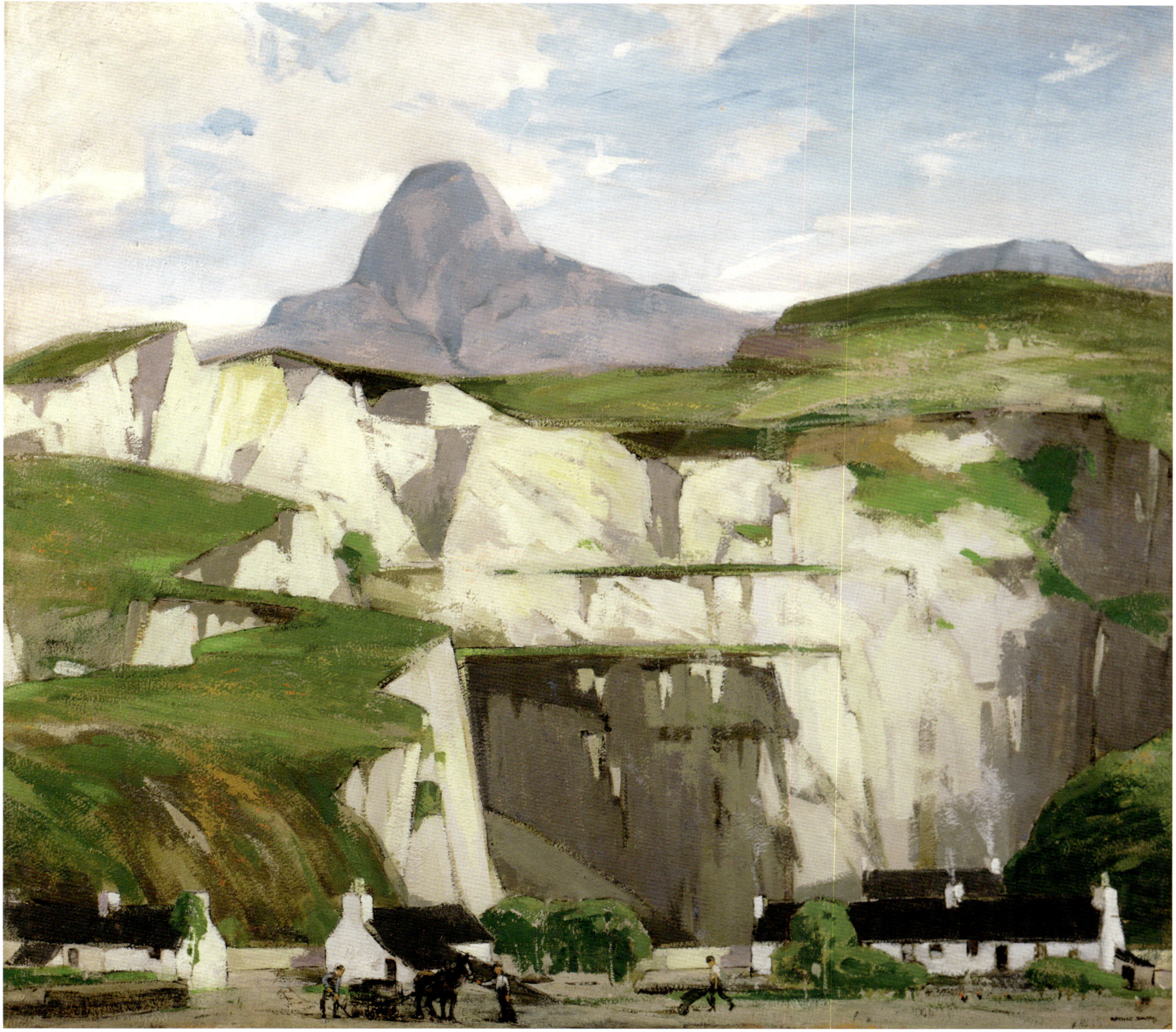

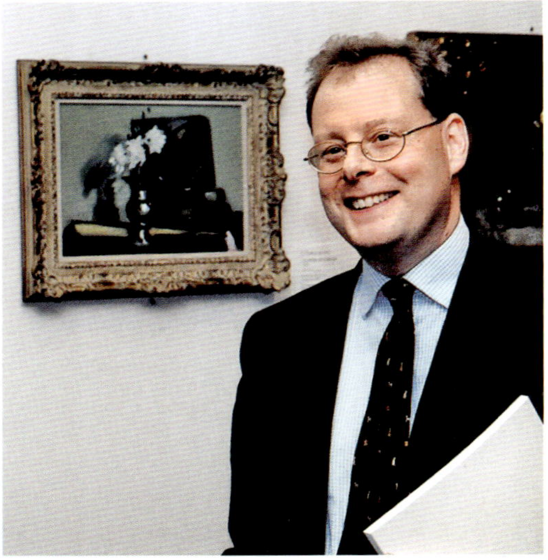

Mungo Campbell worked at the National Galleries of Scotland for twelve years and became Deputy Director at the Hunterian in 1997. He served on the Visual Art Committee of the Scottish Arts Council 1998–2003, chaired the SAC visual arts panels for Exhibition and Educational Awards, is a member of the Visual Arts and Galleries Association Executive and Chair of the Skateraw Foundation Board in East Lothian.

DUNARA CASTLE

FRANCIS CAMPBELL BOILEAU CADELL RSA RSW (1883–1937)

c.1929, oil on millboard, 38.1x45.7 cm

Purchased 1970

'A rare Colourist depiction of the practicalities of Hebridean life, the picture was possibly prompted by a request in April 1929, that Cadell produce a series of images – to include a steamer – for the ferry company, MacBraynes. Although he declined the commission, this work attests to the central place ships have in the life of the west of Scotland. While the startlingly clear light and the white-painted yacht point to the enduring attractions of a summer in the Hebrides, the steamer is seen at one of its many ports of call on its lifeline route plying between Glasgow and St Kilda. Within a year, the *Dunara Castle* helped evacuate the last St Kildans from their isolated home. Many such communities remain as fragile as they were eighty years ago; the trajectory of depopulation and it consequences continues into the twenty-first century.'

– Chosen by Mungo Campbell, Deputy Director, Hunterian Museum and Art Gallery, University of Glasgow.

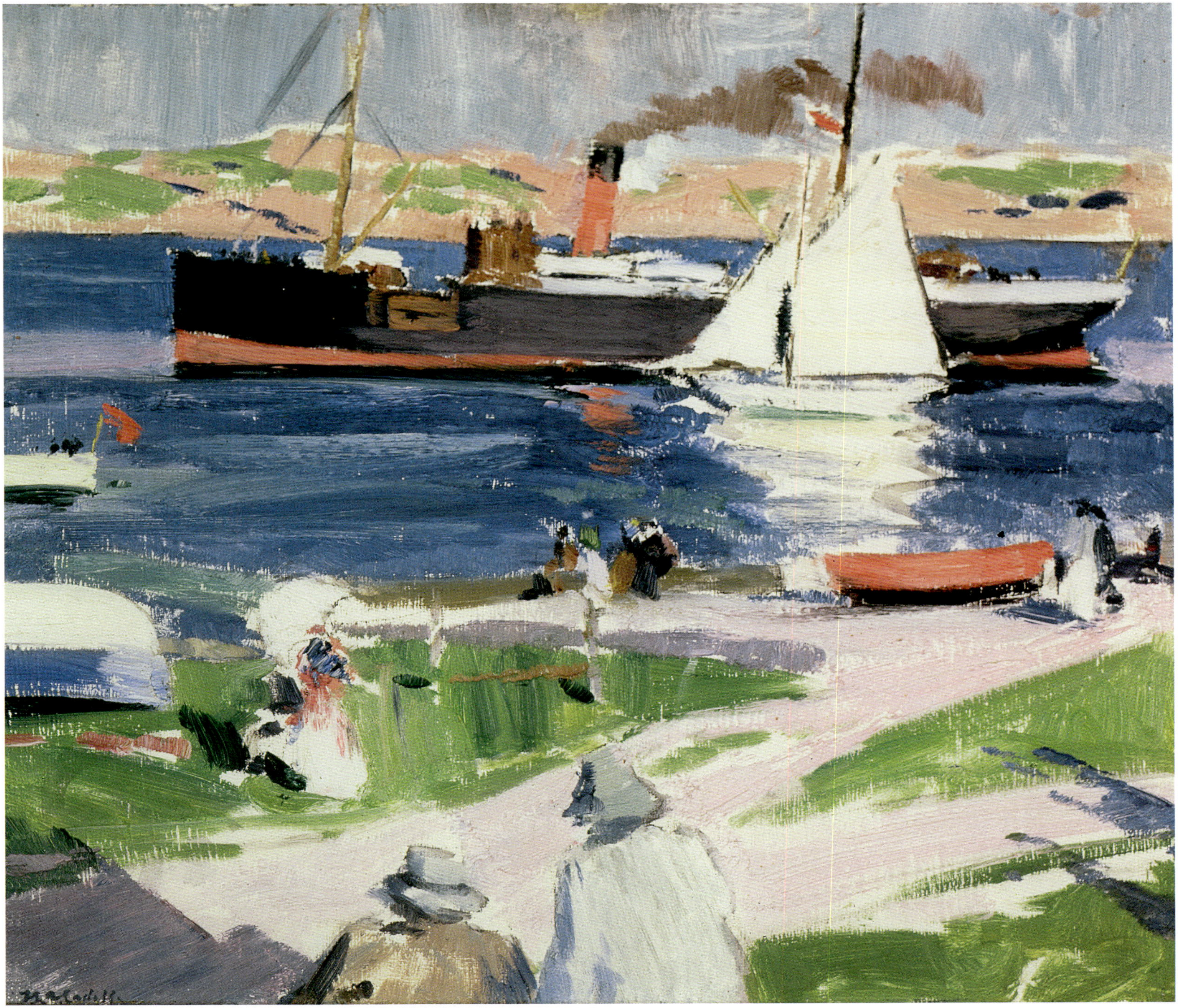

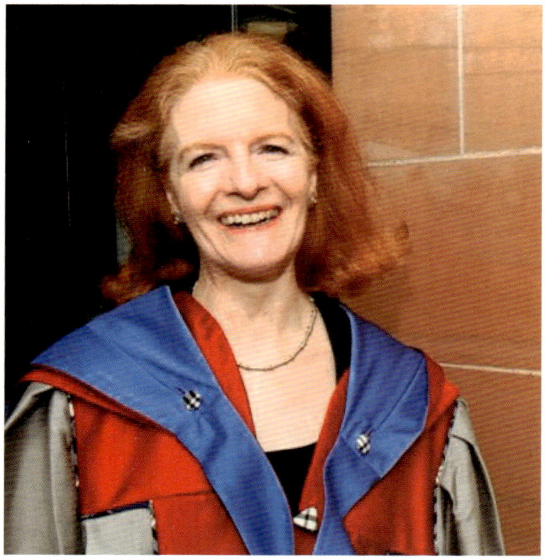

Carol Høgel is one of Scotland's most generous and artistically informed philanthropists. Her family charitable fund, the Dunard Fund, is one of the few key trusts supporting the arts in Scotland. It has provided vital support for, among others, the Edinburgh International Festival, Scottish Opera, the Scottish Chamber Orchestra, the National Galleries of Scotland and the Royal Scottish National Orchestra. In 2008 she was among the first five people to receive the Prince of Wales Medal For Arts Philanthropy.

THE FEATHERED HAT

FRANCIS CAMPBELL BOILEAU CADELL RSA RSW (1883–1937)

c.1915, oil on millboard, 45.7x35.5 cm

Purchased 1992

'I love the artistic license Cadell has chosen – for colour and for balance – of putting the pink rose from the bosom of our sitter into the mirror as a reflection. But how is it possible, given the angle of the sitter, with her back at an acute angle to the mirror, to have the pink rose reflected in that way? It is only possible because with an artist, anything is possible.

I am drawn to the lady, in her hat, because she reminds me of my own grandmother, who always managed to arrange herself comfortably in uncomfortable clothes because she was comfortable with herself and her appearance.'

– Chosen by Carol Høgel CBE.

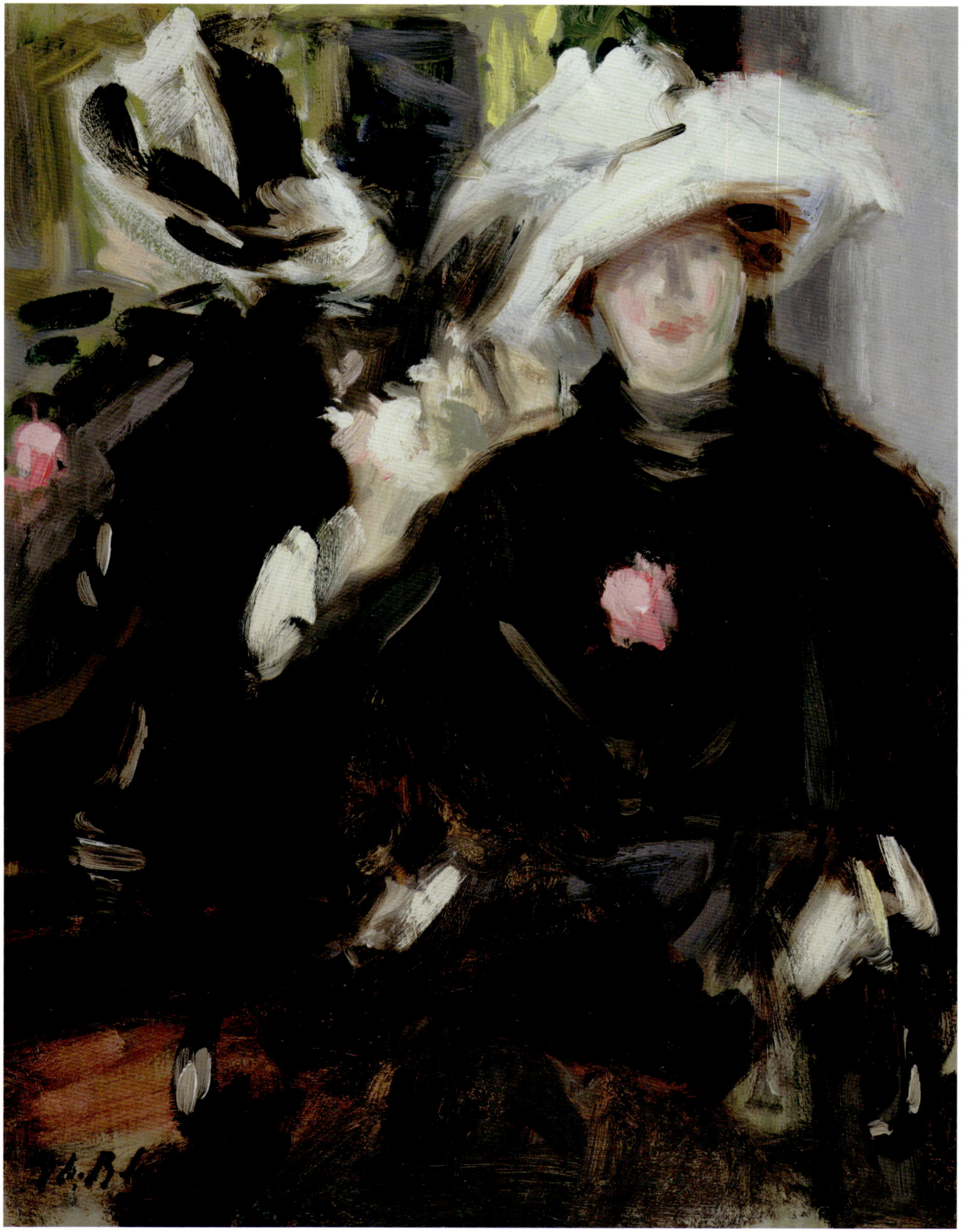

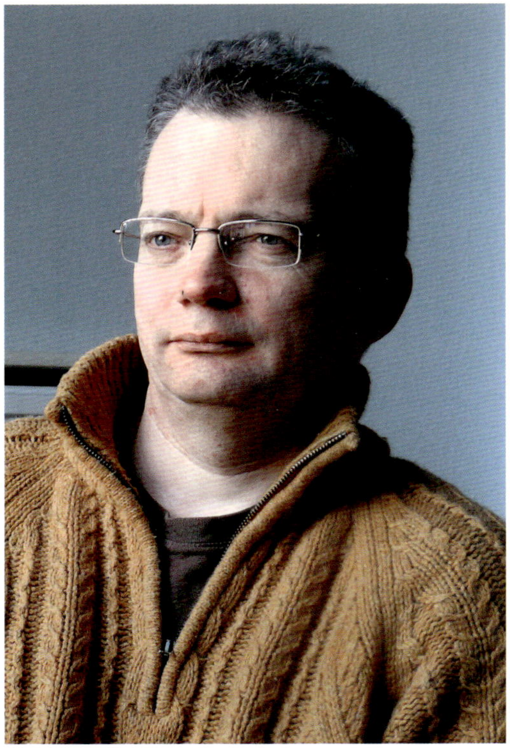

Patrick Elliott grew up in West Sussex. He studied at the Courtauld Institute of Art in London, completing a BA in 1984 and then a PhD on 'Sculpture in France between the Wars'. He has worked as a curator at the Scottish National Gallery of Modern Art in Edinburgh since 1989 and is now Chief Curator. He has organised many exhibitions by artists including Alberto Giacometti, René Magritte, Tracey Emin, Rachel Whiteread, Boyle Family, Picasso's prints and Richard Long. He has written books and catalogues on Giacometti, Alan Davie, William Turnbull, Aristide Maillol and contemporary printmaking. He is currently working on a major exhibition of surrealism, to take place at the Gallery of Modern Art in summer 2010. He lives in Edinburgh with his wife and young daughter.

CARNATIONS

FRANCIS CAMPBELL BOILEAU CADELL RSA RSW (1883–1937)

1913, oil on canvas, 76x63.5 cm

Purchased 1976

'I am not a particular fan of the Scottish Colourists but this picture by Cadell is quietly stunning. Often in Colourist still lifes, you get big, punchy roses or tulips – but here the scene is more nuanced, more ambiguous. It's an unusual subject. There's a little painting (it looks like an early Peploe seascape), a Chinese-type bowl and some carnations almost falling out of a glass. The black object is probably a fan, and next to it is a bit of blue material. The object at the top is ambiguous – it could be a convex mirror, but the reflection doesn't look right. There is no drama here, no centre of focus. Your eye scans it without knowing where to stop. The frame of the picture in the middle (a leitmotif of Cadell's art: he often paints pictures within pictures) gives it structure; the rest of it is seems casual but is perfectly balanced. Painting something like this, where the viewer can't tell exactly what the subject is, requires great skill and confidence; there is always the pernicious temptation to add more detail. I love the way he has painted that blue material, and the shadow under the picture frame is just right: it anchors everything. Even the wall is good. He's in complete command of the picture. It's as good as Manet or early William Nicholson. I'd be very happy to have this picture at home.'

– Chosen by Dr. Patrick Elliott, Chief Curator, Scottish National Gallery of Modern Art.

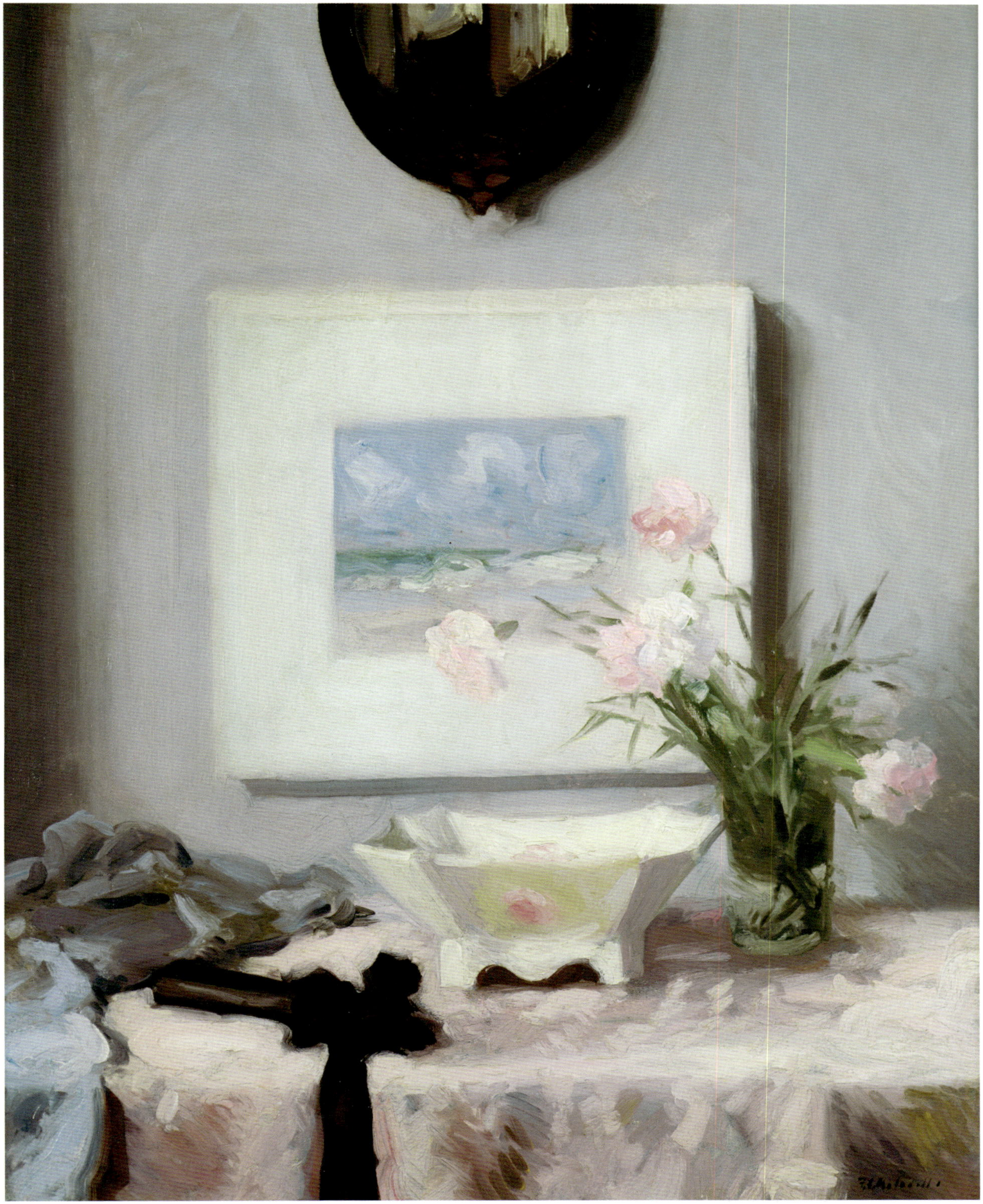

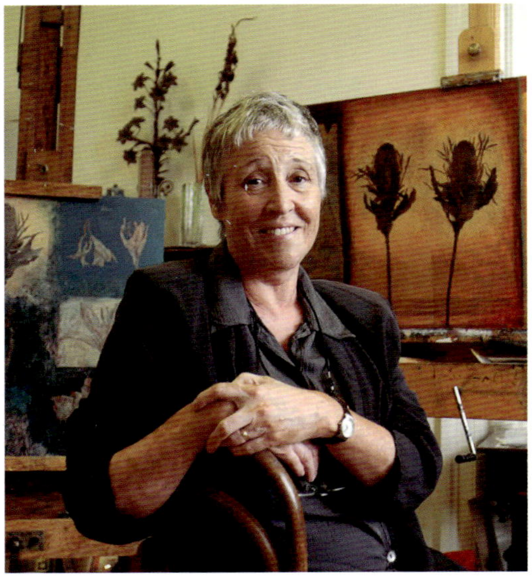

Victoria Crowe studied at Kingston School of Art and the Royal College of Art in London. She has lived in Scotland since 1968, when Sir Robin Philipson invited her to become a part-time lecturer at Edinburgh College of Art, where she taught until 1998. A painter of still lifes, interiors and landscapes, she is also an accomplished portrait painter and her work is represented in a number of public and private collections. An exhibition of her work *A Shepherd's Life, Paintings of Jenny Armstrong* was shown at The Fleming Collection in 2009. Crowe was honoured with a Doctor Honoris Causa from the University of Aberdeen in the same year.

SELF-PORTRAIT WITH THE ARTIST'S FIRST WIFE

JAMES COWIE RSA (1886–1956)

1923, oil on canvas, 62x62 cm

Purchased 2008

'I love the luminosity of this painting; it has a still and timeless quality. Criticized as backward looking, it was Cowie's very adherence to traditional values and artistic skills which enabled him to make work dealing with our very contemporary concerns of psychological tensions within a painting and how we interpret the 'reality' of the external world.

To me this painting depicts an intimate insight into a marriage at a portentous time. The figures make a united whole, her hands clasped round her pregnant belly, echoing the line of his leaning back, and her concentrated gaze on what seems to be the very canvas Cowie's self portrait is being painted on. I feel I am looking at the painting, meeting Cowie's outward gaze, but I also acknowledge that I am seeing what she saw, – a strange interaction made all the more intense by the artist's use of the confines of stretcher and coombed wall.'

– Chosen by Victoria Crowe OBE RSA RSW, Artist.

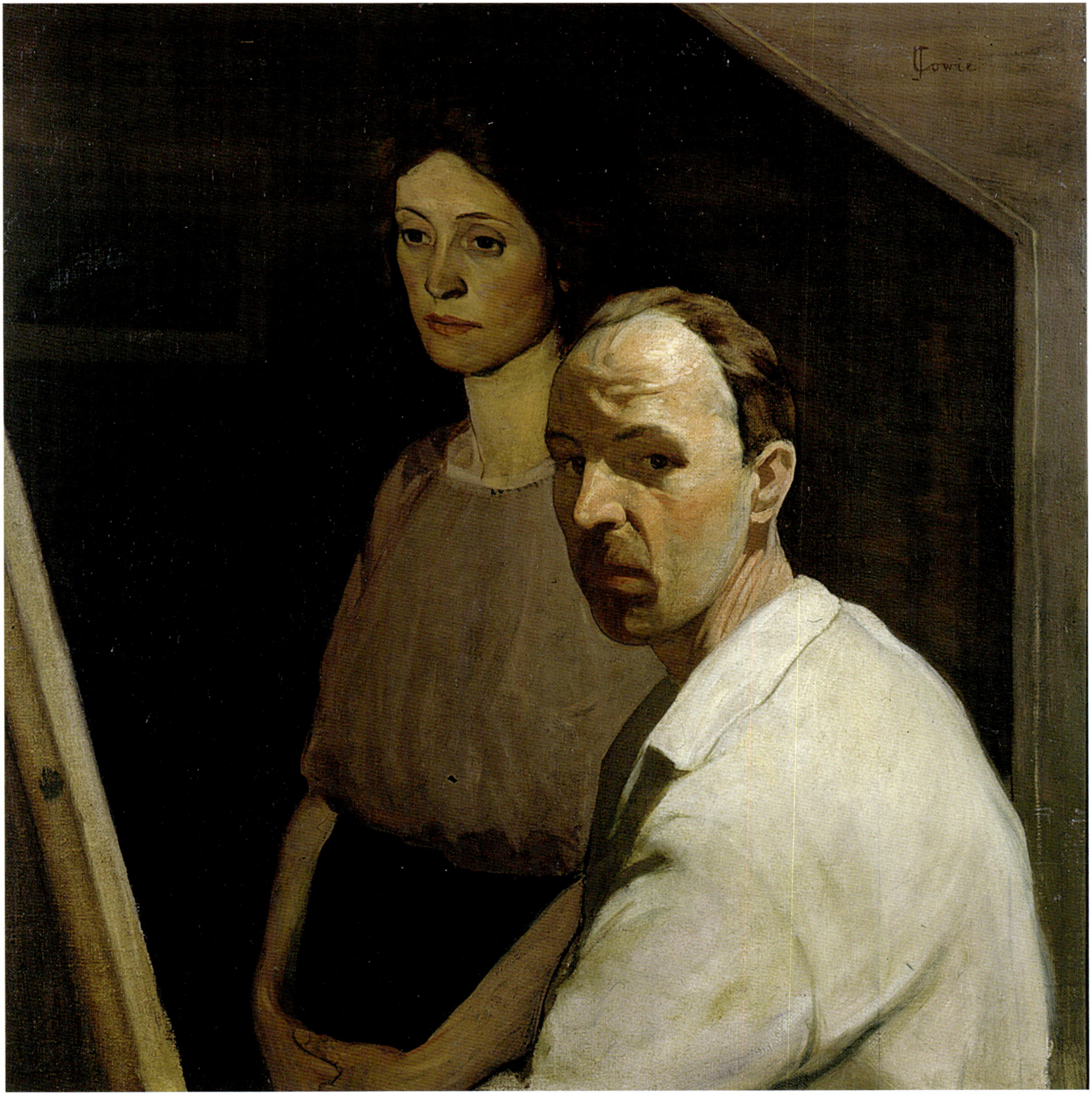
Cowie

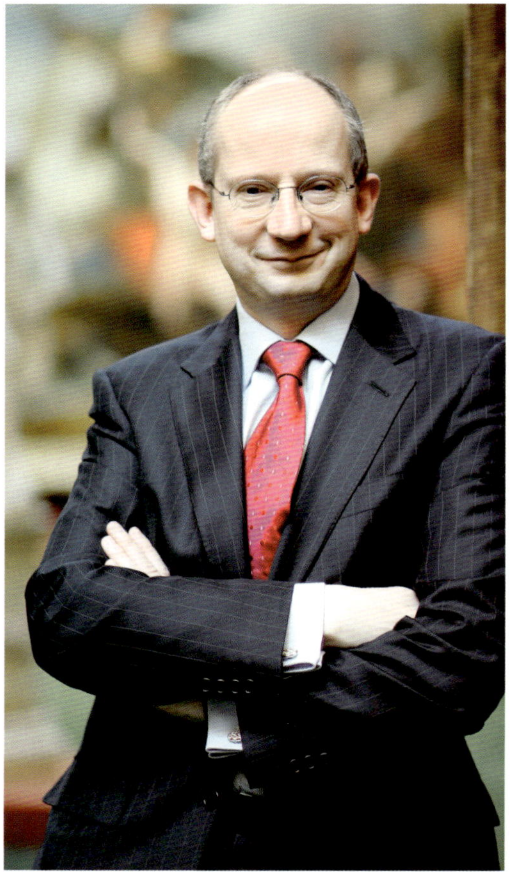

John Leighton was born in Belfast and studied Fine Art at the University of Edinburgh and Edinburgh College of Art and History of Art at the Courtauld Institute of Art. He worked as Curator of nineteenth-century paintings at the National Gallery in London and was Director of the Van Gogh Museum from 1997 until his appointment as Director-General of the National Galleries of Scotland in March 2006. Leighton has curated numerous exhibitions including Caspar David Friedrich's *Winter Landscapes* (1990), *Art in the Making: Impressionism* (1990), *Seurat's Bathers* (1997), *Signac* (2001) and *Manet and the Sea* (2004). He has contributed to the catalogues for the above exhibitions and published and lectured on various aspects of nineteenth and twentieth-century art.

RECLINING LADY IN WHITE

STANLEY CURSITER CBE RSA RSW LLD (1887–1976)

oil on panel, 26.7x36.8 cm

Purchased 1982

'Stanley Cursiter was Director of the National Galleries of Scotland from 1930 to 1948. As a museum professional, he was a visionary whose ideas were often ahead of his time. He played a leading role in the campaign to establish a modern art gallery in Edinburgh and was instrumental in introducing key figures of the modern movement to Scotland, including Van Gogh and Matisse. But this versatile Orcadian was also an extremely talented painter. This small study is in some respects a homage to the French painter Manet. But we can also sense the artist's pleasure in sketching with vigorous strokes of a brush loaded with paint and his delight in evoking rather than describing the play of light across the draperies. In these days of increasing specialisation, Cursiter's picture is a useful reminder that it is not a bad thing for an art historian and a museum curator to know one end of paint brush from the other.'

– Chosen by John Leighton, Director-General, National Galleries of Scotland.

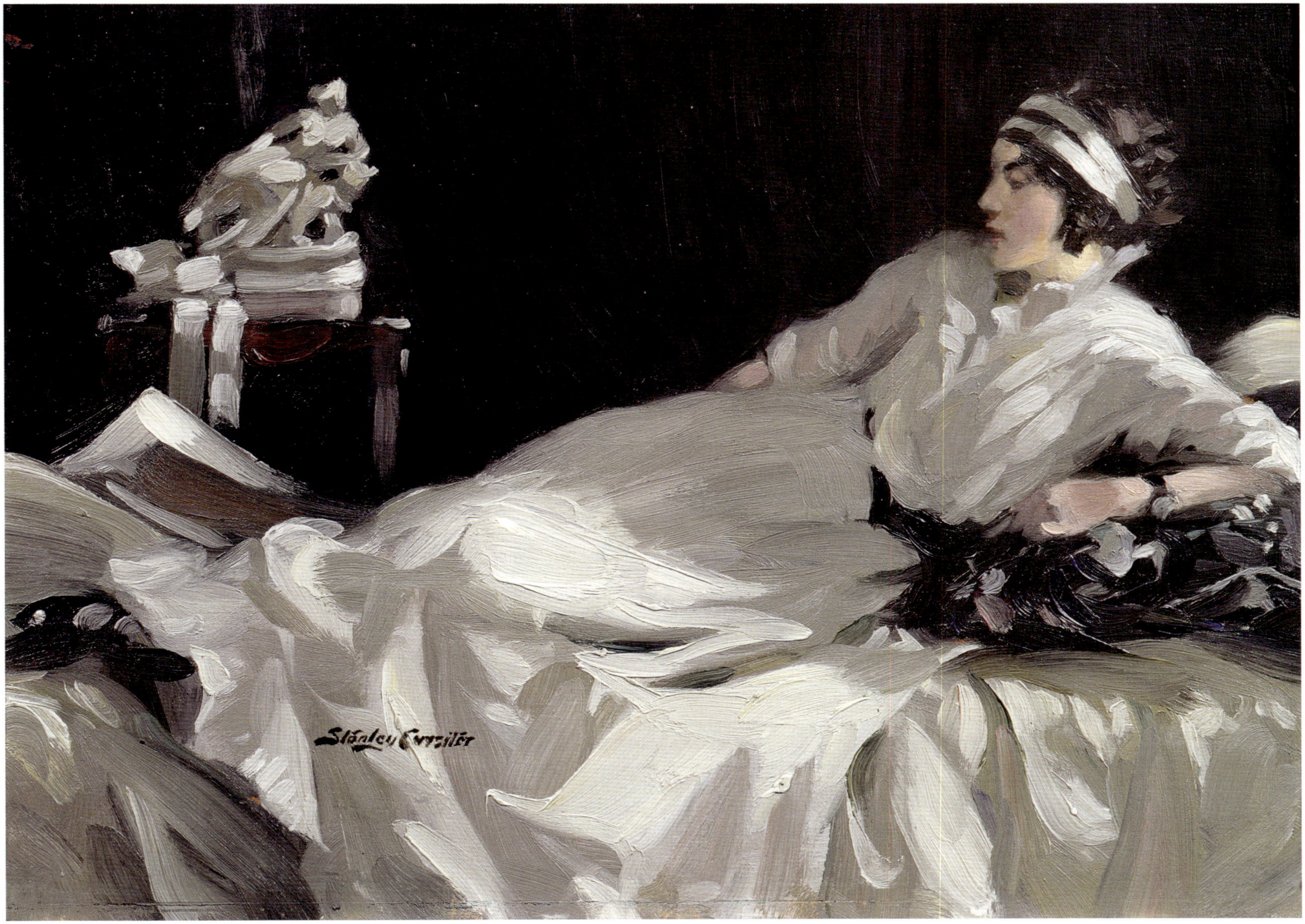
Stanley Cursiter

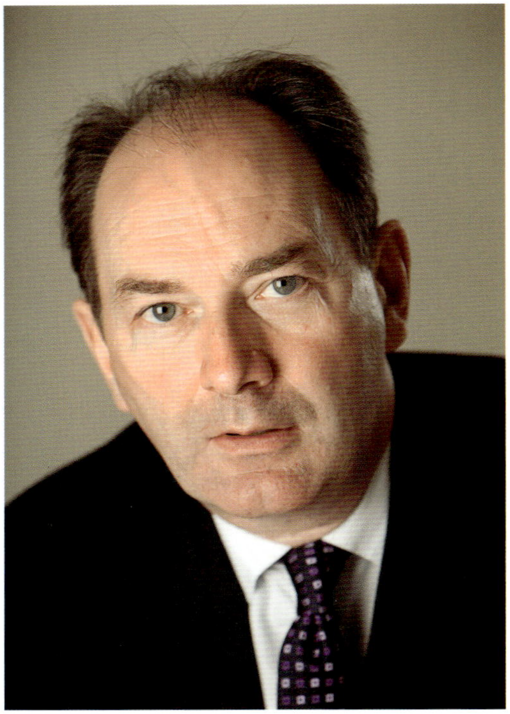

Lord Forsyth served in Government for more than a decade as Secretary of State for Scotland, as a Minister of State at the Home Office and Department of Employment and as Parliamentary Private Secretary to the Foreign Secretary. Before joining Evercore Partners he was a Director of Corporate Finance at Flemings, Vice Chairman Investment Banking Europe at JPMorgan and Deputy Chairman in JPMorgan UK. He is a Non Executive Director of J&J Denholm Ltd and of the Centre for Policy Studies and chaired the Tax Reform Commission. He is a member of the House of Lords Select Committee on Economic Affairs. He was nominated to the Privy Council in 1995, knighted in 1997 and appointed a Life Peer in 1999.

THE EVE OF THE BATTLE OF THE SOMME

SIR HERBERT JAMES GUNN RA (1893–1964)

1916, oil on canvas, 83.8x91.4 cm

Purchased 1995

'I find this picture deeply moving. It is full of symbolism – the young man lying stretched out as if crucified, the disembodied head, the field ambulances in the background are all portents of the catastrophe to come. I believe it was painted by Gunn whilst he was serving in the Great War. He captures the horrors of the war and the terrible toll it would take on a generation of young men. We can still feel some of the consequences of that toll today and this picture for me is a poignant reminder of the debt we owe to our servicemen and women.'

– Chosen by The Rt Hon Lord Forsyth of Drumlean, Senior Managing Director, Evercore Partners.

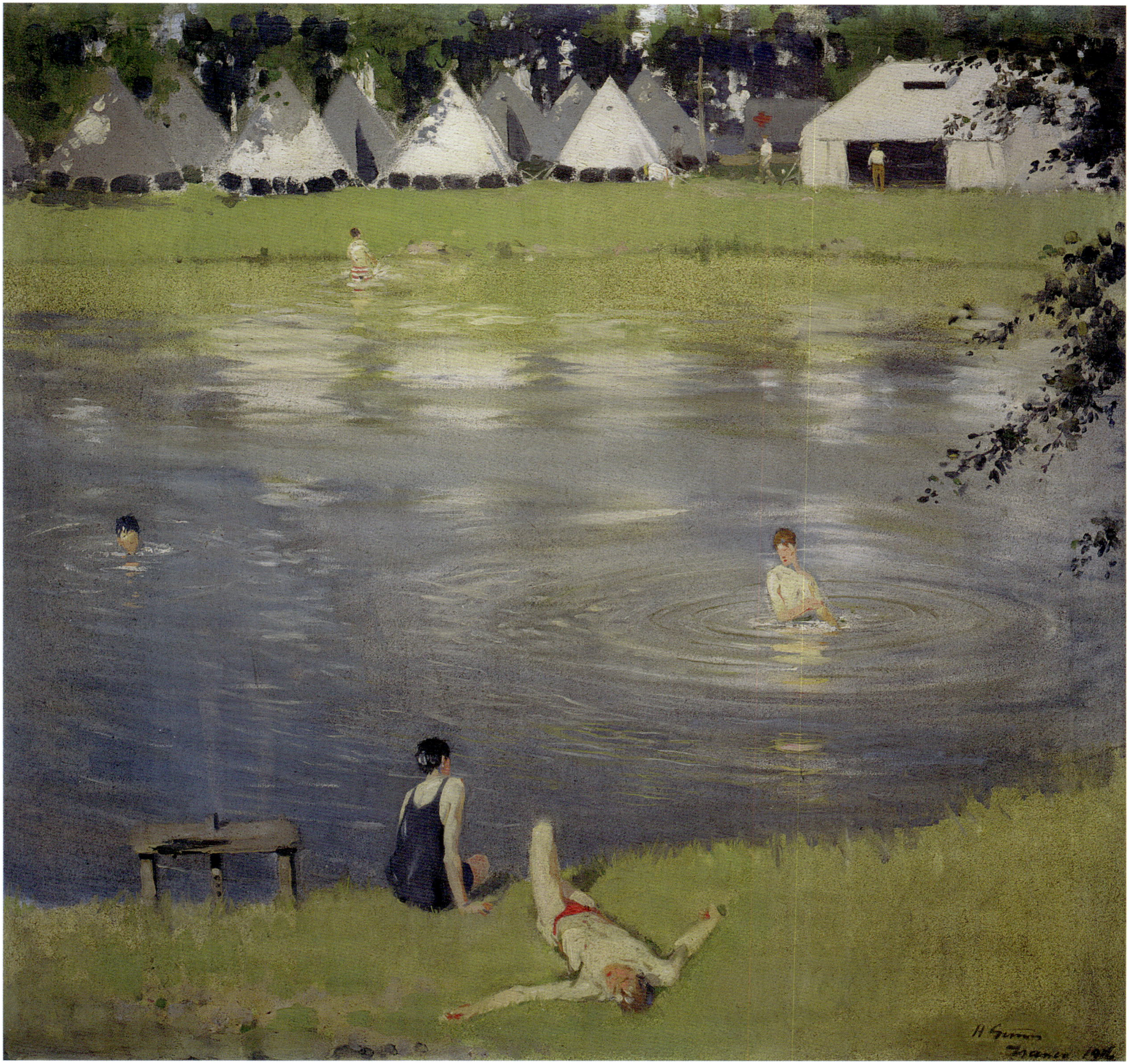
H Gunn
France 1916

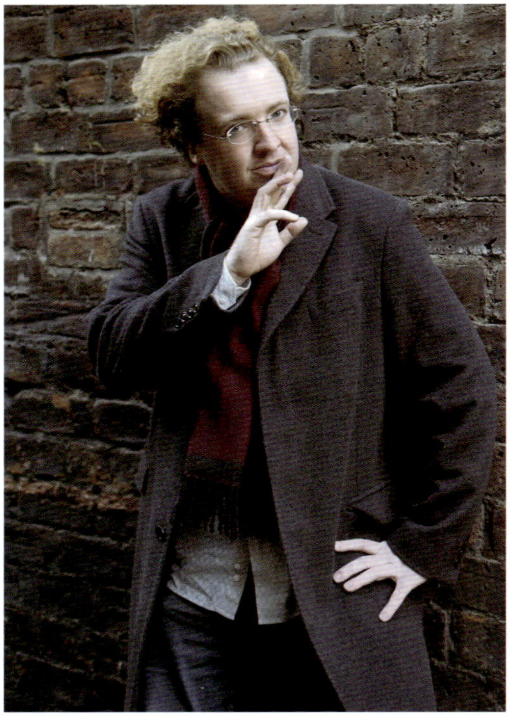

Stéphane Denève was awarded a unanimous first prize when he graduated from the Paris Conservatoire. He became Music Director of the Royal Scottish National Orchestra (RSNO) in 2005. A champion of the music of his native France, premiering new work by young French composers with the RSNO, he works as a guest conductor world-wide. In 2010 he conducted the RSNO in Paris for the first time on a European tour.

STILL LIFE WITH ORANGE CHAIR

ANNE REDPATH OBE RSA ARA ARWS (1895–1965)

Mid-1940s, oil on board, 73.7x53.5 cm

Purchased 1980

'Being French, I am attracted by colours and I adore the Impressionists' time in Paris. Scotland has the Colourists and you would think I would choose one of them but I chose a painting by Anne Redpath: *Still Life with Orange Chair*. It's Post-Impressionist, like Pierre Bonnard, and full of different textures and patterns and I'm fascinated by how those resonate together.

What I find fascinating with Post-Impressionists is that they impress your eye in a certain way so they glow. I often have a test whereby when I leave a gallery I quickly look at each painting to see if one glows more than the others. It's all very subjective of course, but this work by Anne Redpath seems to have this harmonious combination of colours. It's in one dimension, there's no real depth or perspective and I like that because it gives even greater play between the colours. It is similar to works by my beloved Pierre Bonnard, one of my favourite French painters.'

– Chosen by Stéphane Denève, Music Director, Royal Scottish National Orchestra.

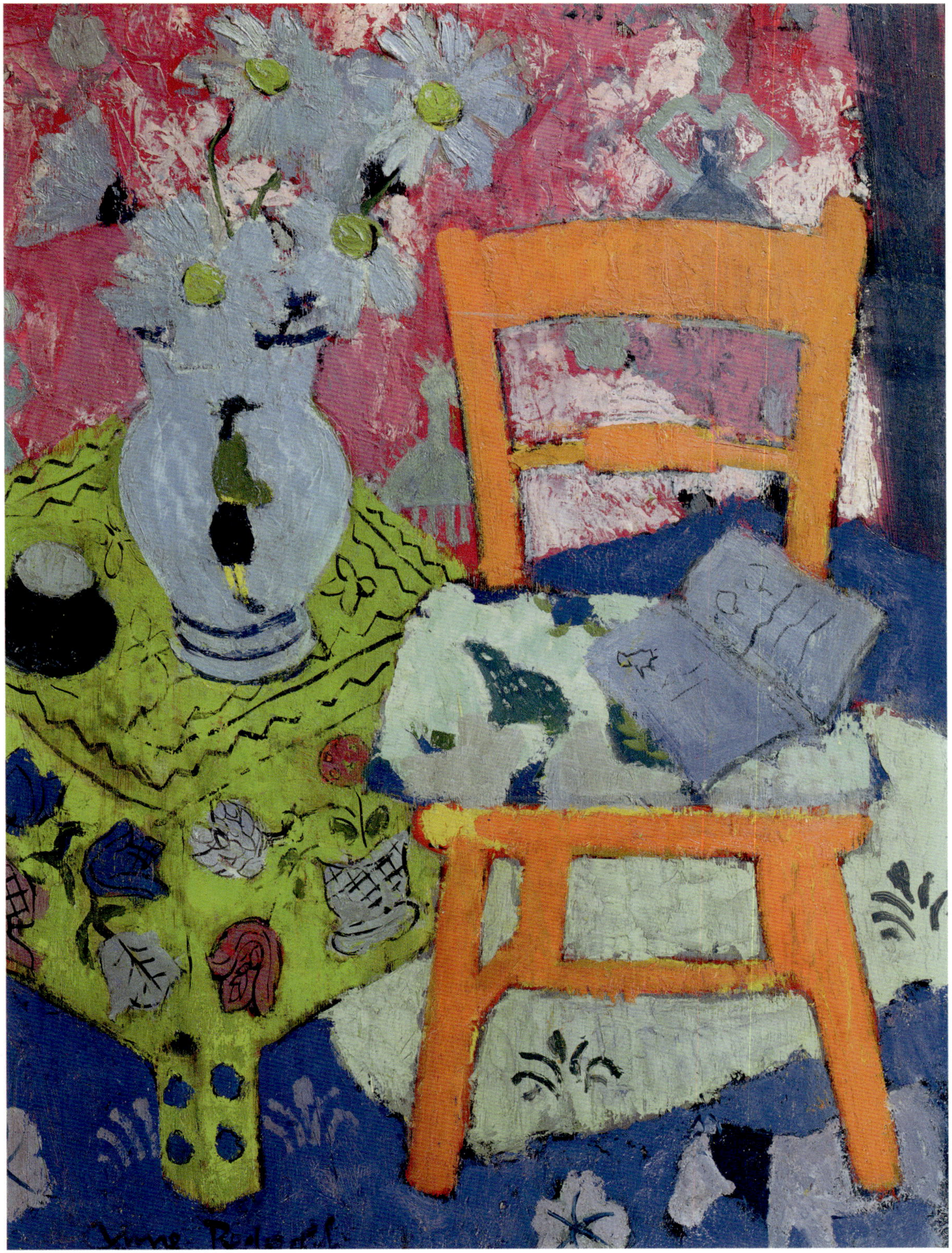

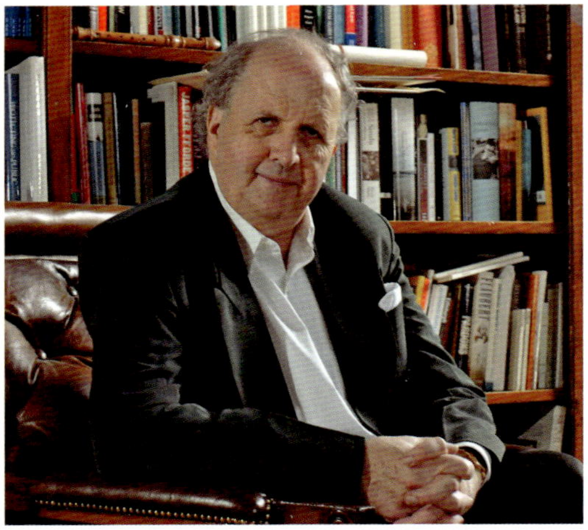

Alexander McCall Smith is the author of over sixty books on a wide array of subjects. For many years he was Professor of Medical Law at the University of Edinburgh and served on national and international bioethics bodies. Then in 1999 he achieved global recognition for his award-winning *No. 1 Ladies' Detective Agency* series, and thereafter devoted his time to the writing of fiction, including the *44 Scotland Street* and the *von Igelfeld* series. His books have been translated into forty-two languages. He lives in Edinburgh with his wife Elizabeth, a doctor.

WINDOW AT MENTON

ANNE REDPATH OBE RSA ARA ARWS (1895–1965)

1948, oil on plywood, 109.2x83.8 cm

Purchased 1992

'What I like about Anne Redpath's paintings is their intimacy. *Window in Menton* reminds me of a Pierre Bonnard interior both in the colours which the artist uses and in the figure's preoccupation with something in front of her. This is a very domestic moment and I think that it takes a particular skill to capture that. Bonnard certainly had it, as did Vuillard; Redpath is, I think, quite worthy of being mentioned in such company.

There are other interesting things happening here. The perspective is odd. I have been told that this may be because she was influenced by the Pre-Modern perspective that she saw in Sienese paintings when she went to Siena as a young woman. I went to study in Siena many years ago and I remember being very taken with those lovely, rather flat paintings of the Sienese school. Then there is the open window. I love a painting with an open window.'

– Chosen by Alexander McCall Smith, Author.

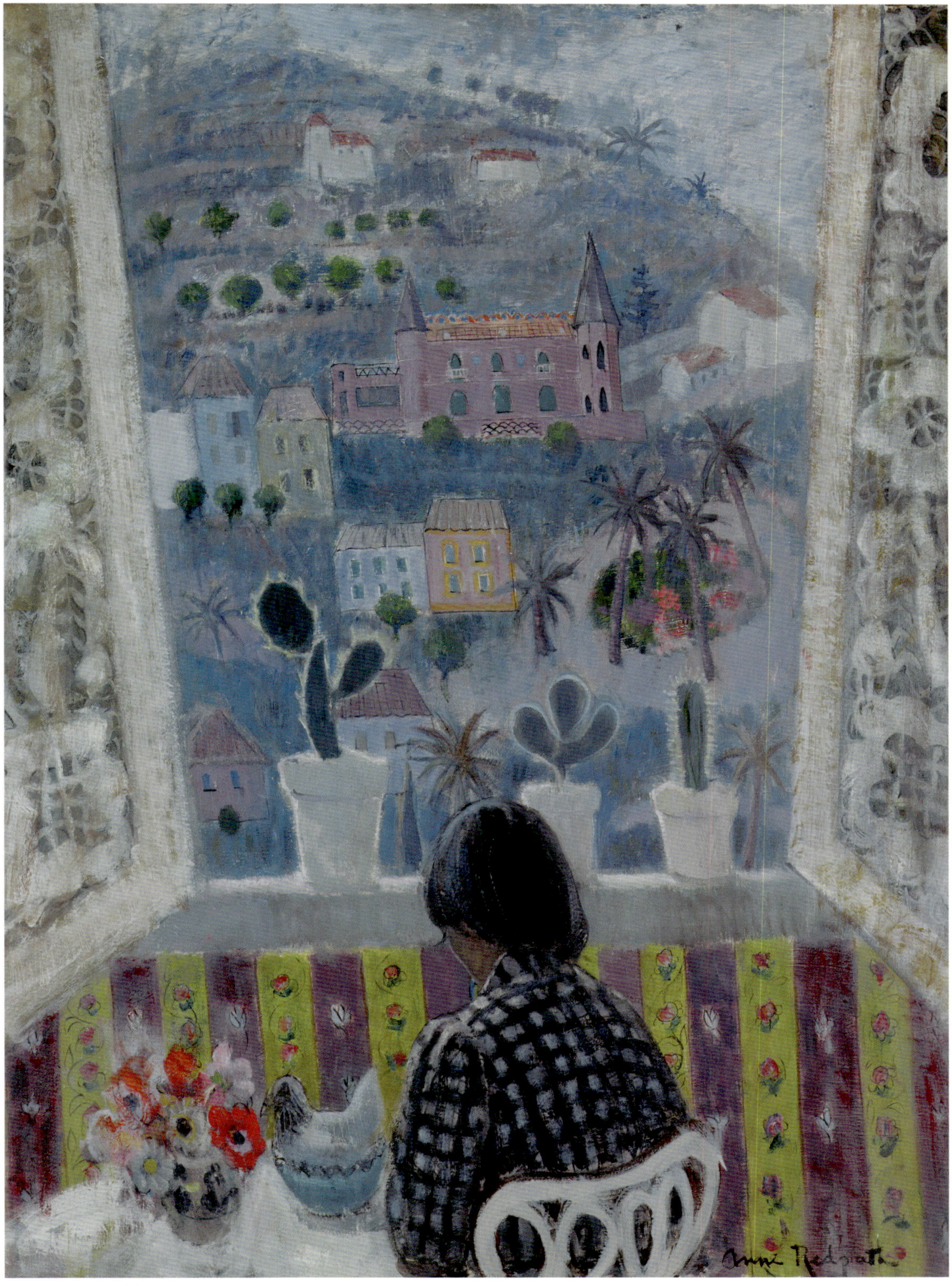

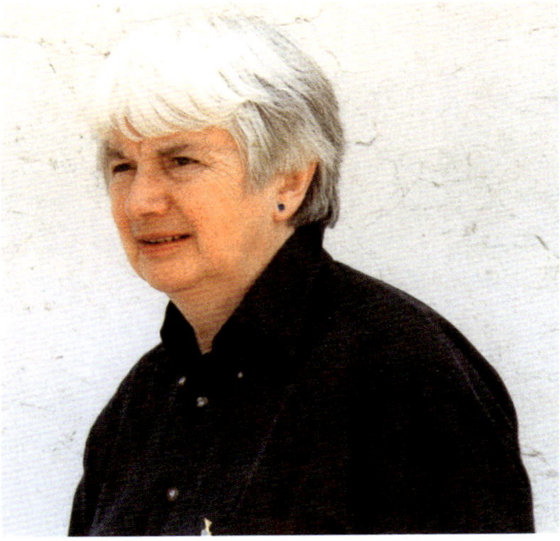

Dame Elizabeth Blackadder studied Fine Art at the University of Edinburgh and Edinburgh College of Art (ECA), graduating with First Class Honours in 1954. She married fellow artist John Houston in 1956. Blackadder lectured at ECA from1963 retiring in1986. Since she received the Andrew Carnegie travelling scholarship from the Royal Scottish Academy in 1954 extensive travel in Europe, North America and Japan has informed her work. She is a prolific painter and printmaker and her broad skills base has resulted in commissions for tapestry design, a painted window and Royal Mail postage stamps. Blackadder is the first woman to be elected an Academician of the Royal Scottish Academy and the Royal Academy, London. She has also received Honorary Doctorates from four Scottish universities. In 2001 she was appointed Her Majesty's Painter and Limner in Scotland. Blackadder lives and works in Edinburgh.

ANSTRUTHER

SIR WILLIAM GEORGE GILLIES RA RSA PRSW (1898–1973)

1946, oil on canvas, 41.9x51.4 cm

Purchased 1976

'A small canvas but it says everything – the rocks, the walls, houses, sea and sky all have a completeness, everything has been said about this corner of a Fife harbour – with the movement of the sea and the light. I love the simplicity of the vision and the marvellous quality and handling of the paint.'

– Chosen by Dame Elizabeth Blackadder DBE RA RSA RSW, Artist.

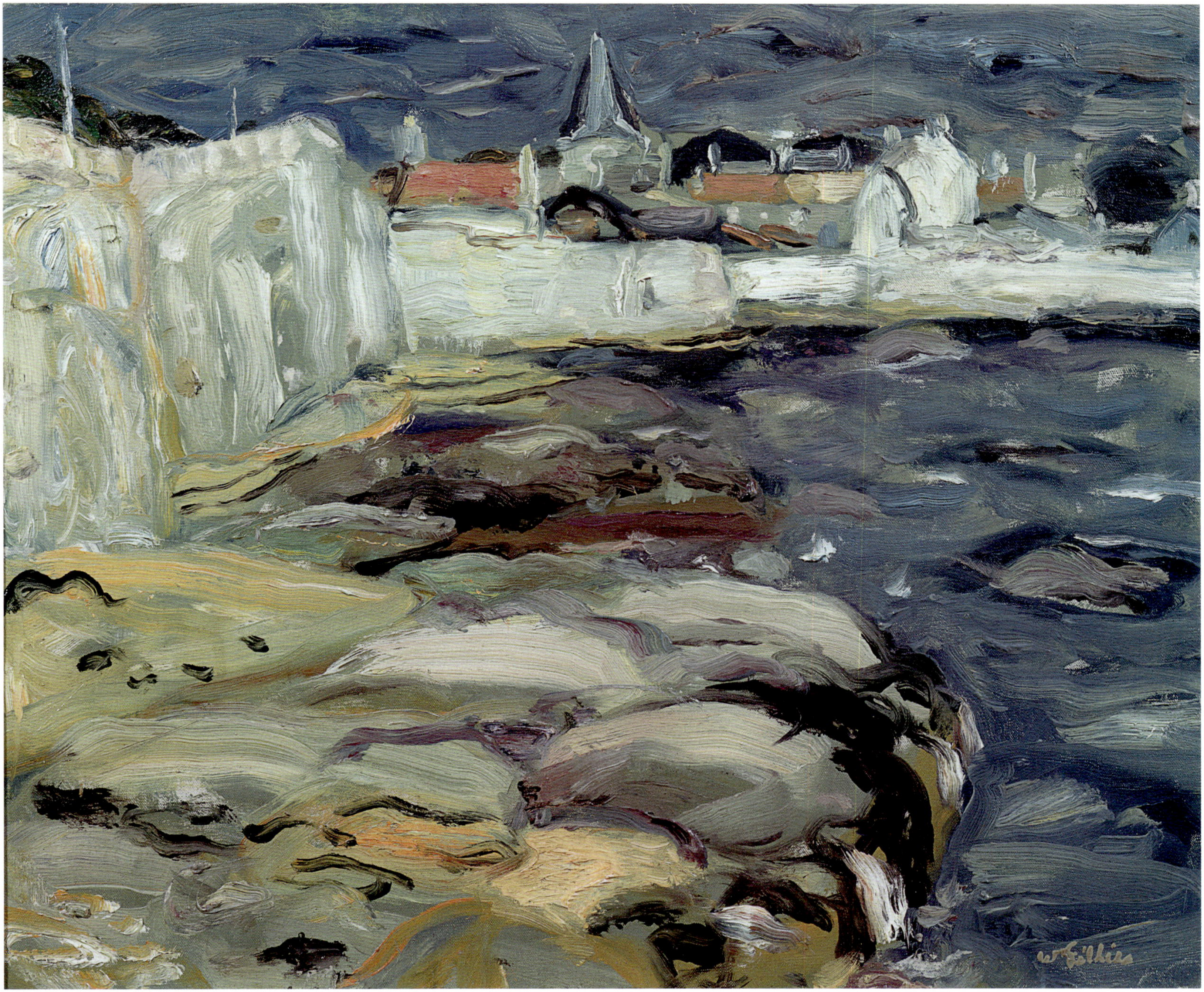

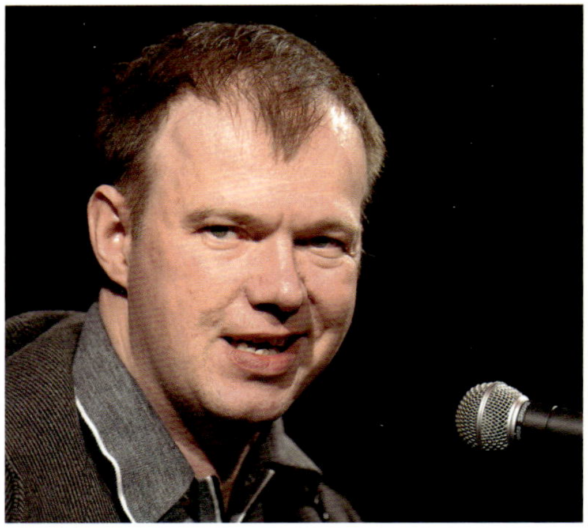

Edwyn Collins was born in Edinburgh and formed the musical group Nu-Sonics in 1976, which became Orange Juice in 1979. Critically admired within independent rock circles, Orange Juice are perhaps best known for their no.8 UK Top 40 single, *Rip It Up*. In 1985, Orange Juice disbanded, and Collins has since then pursued a solo career. In 2005, a severe stroke left Collins unable to walk, talk, or even play the guitar. In 2007, he returned for his first stage performance. His first new track since the stroke, *I'm Feeling Lucky*, a song written with his son William, was released in February 2010. Collins performed at The Fleming Collection in 2009.

ROSS-SHIRE LANDSCAPE NEAR POOLEWE

JAMES MCINTOSH PATRICK RSA ROI ARE (1907–1998)

1939, oil on canvas, 29.2x45.1cm

Purchased 1984

'I knew the artist when I was quite a young boy. My father and he were on the staff at Duncan of Jordanstone Art School in Dundee. I gave him a picture I drew of a barn owl. Later he gave my mother a watercolour for me. I have it still, a treasured possession. He was very kind, a great talker. He liked that I was compellingly interested in wildlife, especially birds, my boyhood passion. He was an old man in his sixties, but we had a friendly relationship.

Looking at this painting I see his fanciful view of nature, somewhat stylised. I like to draw like that now, not so naturalistic. I know a lot of his work and feel an understanding of it.'

– Chosen by Edwyn Collins, Musician.

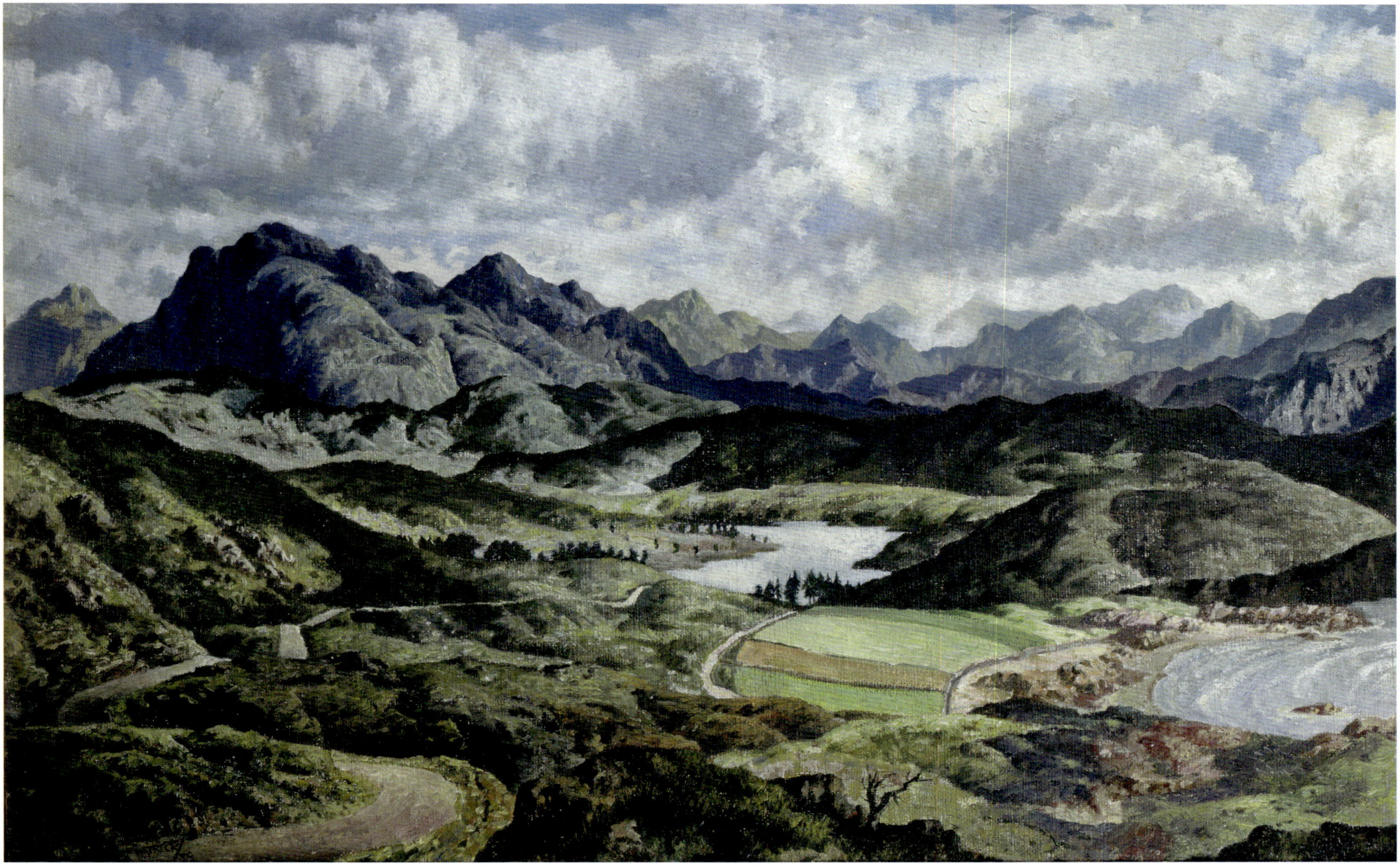

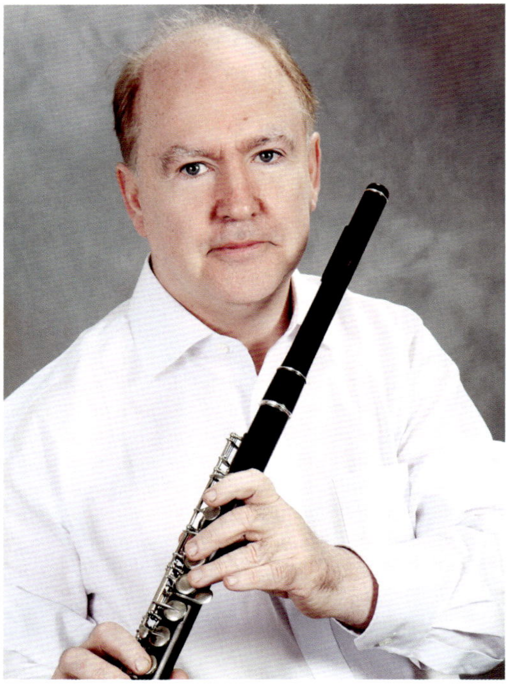

In 2006 the Cheltenham Music Festival was assigned a Scottish theme and an opportunity arose for four well-known Scottish composers, David Horne, Anna Meredith, Alasdair Nicholson and **Eddie McGuire** to explore The Fleming Collection. The four resulting compositions or *Scottish Miniatures,* together with interludes by David Horne, formed one piece performed by The Scottish Chamber Orchestra on Saturday 8th July 2006 conducted by Joseph Swensen. This world premier of *Scottish Miniatures* was broadcast by BBC Radio 3 four days later. To compliment the concert a touring exhibition of paintings from The Fleming Collection curated by Dr Cecilia Powell entitled *The Scottishness of Scottish Art: The Fleming Collection* was shown at the Cheltenham Museum and Art Gallery.

RAG AND BONE SHOP, GLASGOW

JOAN EARDLEY RSA (1921–1963)

watercolour, 33x26.6 cm

Purchased 1988

'My piece *Junk Shop Blues* – for the Scottish Chamber Orchestra – was inspired by Joan Eardley's painting *Rag and Bone Shop*. Seeing it struck a chord of early childhood memories in my heart. She had moved to my home town, Glasgow, at the start of the Second World War, with her mother, to study at the Glasgow School of Art, and her depictions of post-war urban life there parallel my own efforts in such works as *A Glasgow Symphony*. I knew 'rag and bone shops' as 'junk shops', and became fascinated by them on visits (at first with my mother) in the 1950s city. With hints of jig rhythm and the Glasgow jazz revival of the time, and brief references to three street songs, a symphonic study evolved expressing a close affinity with Joan's watercolour.'

– Chosen by Eddie McGuire, Composer.

For the Cheltenham Music Festival 2006 David Horne chose JOHN DUNCAN RSA RSW (1886–1945) THE TURN OF THE TIDE; Alasdair Nicolson chose PHILIP REEVES RSA PRSW (b.1931) VAPOUR TRAIL OVER THE HILL; Anna Meredith chose CHARLES RENNIE MACKINTOSH (1868–1928) BUTTERFLY FLOWER, BOWLING.

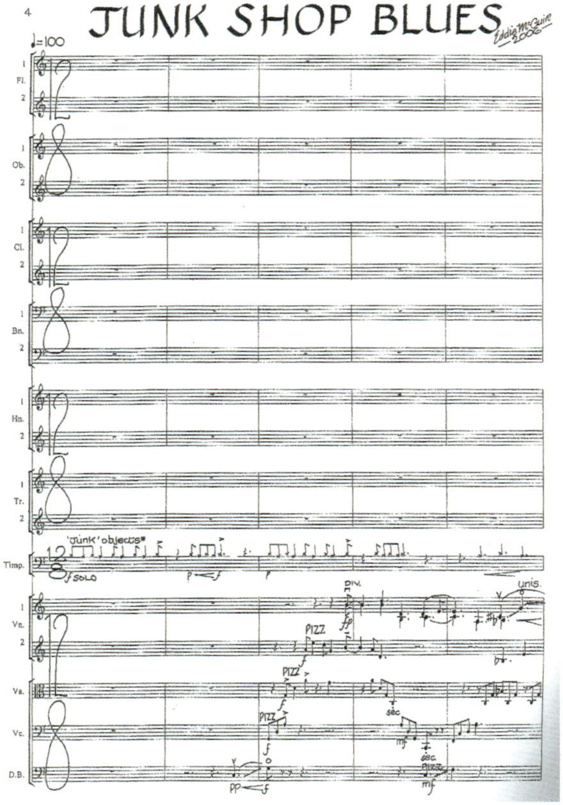
JUNK SHOP BLUES
♩=100
Fl.
Ob.
Cl.
Bn.
Hn.
Tr.
Timp.
'junk' objects*
Vn.
Va.
Vc.
D.B.
pizz
unis.

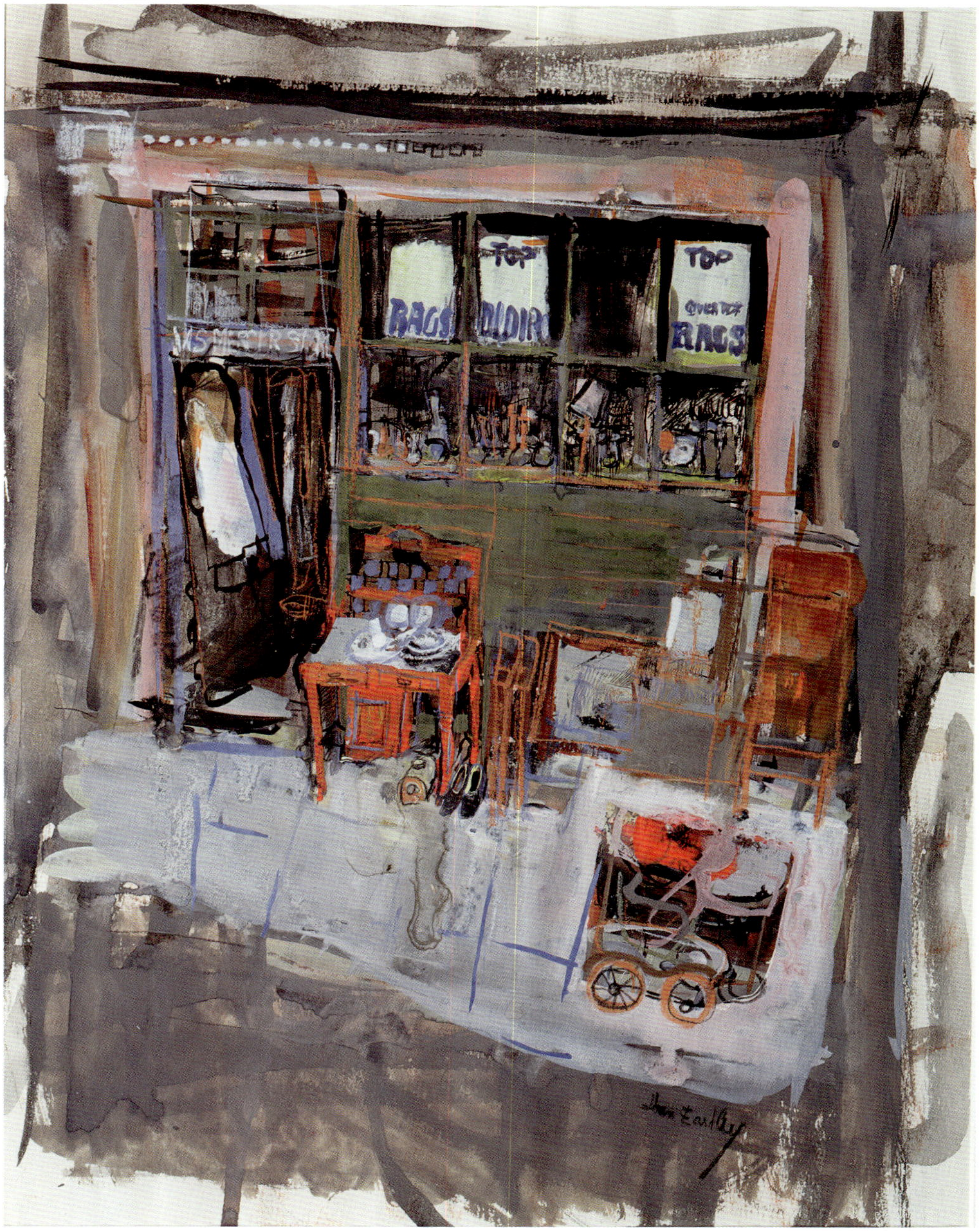
TOP
RAGS
TOP
RAGS

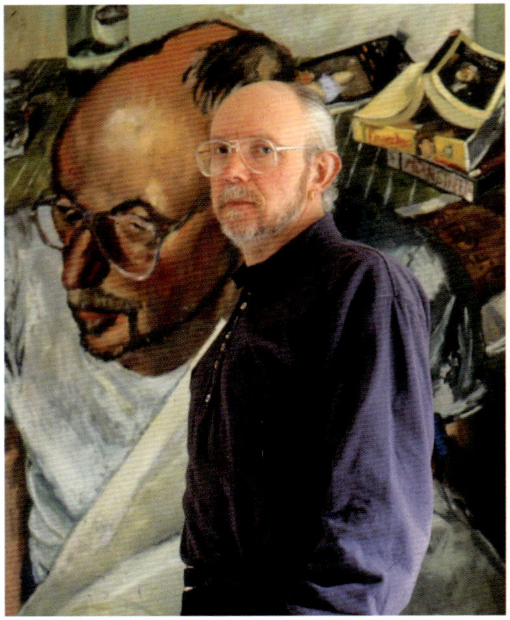

Bill Hare studied Art History at the University of Edinburgh and the Courtauld Institute in London. He was Exhibition Organiser at the Talbot Rice Gallery, Edinburgh until 1995 and since then has concentrated on teaching and curating, with a special interest in post-war Scottish art. He is now an Honorary Teaching Fellow in Scottish art history at Edinburgh University and Honorary Curator of the University's Fine Art Collection. He has curated many exhibitions both in Britain and abroad including two important thematic exhibitions – *Divided Selves: The Scottish Self-Portrait from the 17th Century to the Present* (2006) and *Beyond Appearances: Painting and Picturing in Scottish Modern and Contemporary Painting* (2007). Throughout his career he has published extensively on Scottish modern art and is the author of *Contemporary Painting in Scotland* (1992) and a new monograph on Barbara Rae. He is a board member for Art in Healthcare and a member of the International Association of Art Critics.

CRUCIFIXION

CRAIGIE AITCHISON CBE RA (1926–2009)

1993, oil on canvas, 121.9x121.9 cm

Purchased 1995

'This truly pure and simple image is one of the many versions which the artist has continued to paint on the universal theme of crucifixion since his student days at the Slade in the early 1950s. Although this iconic subject was central to European art before the period of modernism it has rarely be attempted over the last century. Thus what is so startling about this painting is the apparent ease with which the artist has harmoniously integrated the religious spirit of Christian art, going back to Giotto and Piero, with the pictorial language of modern decorative painting. Furthermore, the painter, through a composition of austere intensity and a finely balanced arrangement of evocative colour harmonies, miraculously concentrates into one enthralling image the unbreakable bond of love and devotion between the eternal presence of the divine and a world forever in need of redemption and salvation.'

– Chosen by Bill Hare, Honorary Fellow, The University of Edinburgh, Lecturer, Writer, Curator.

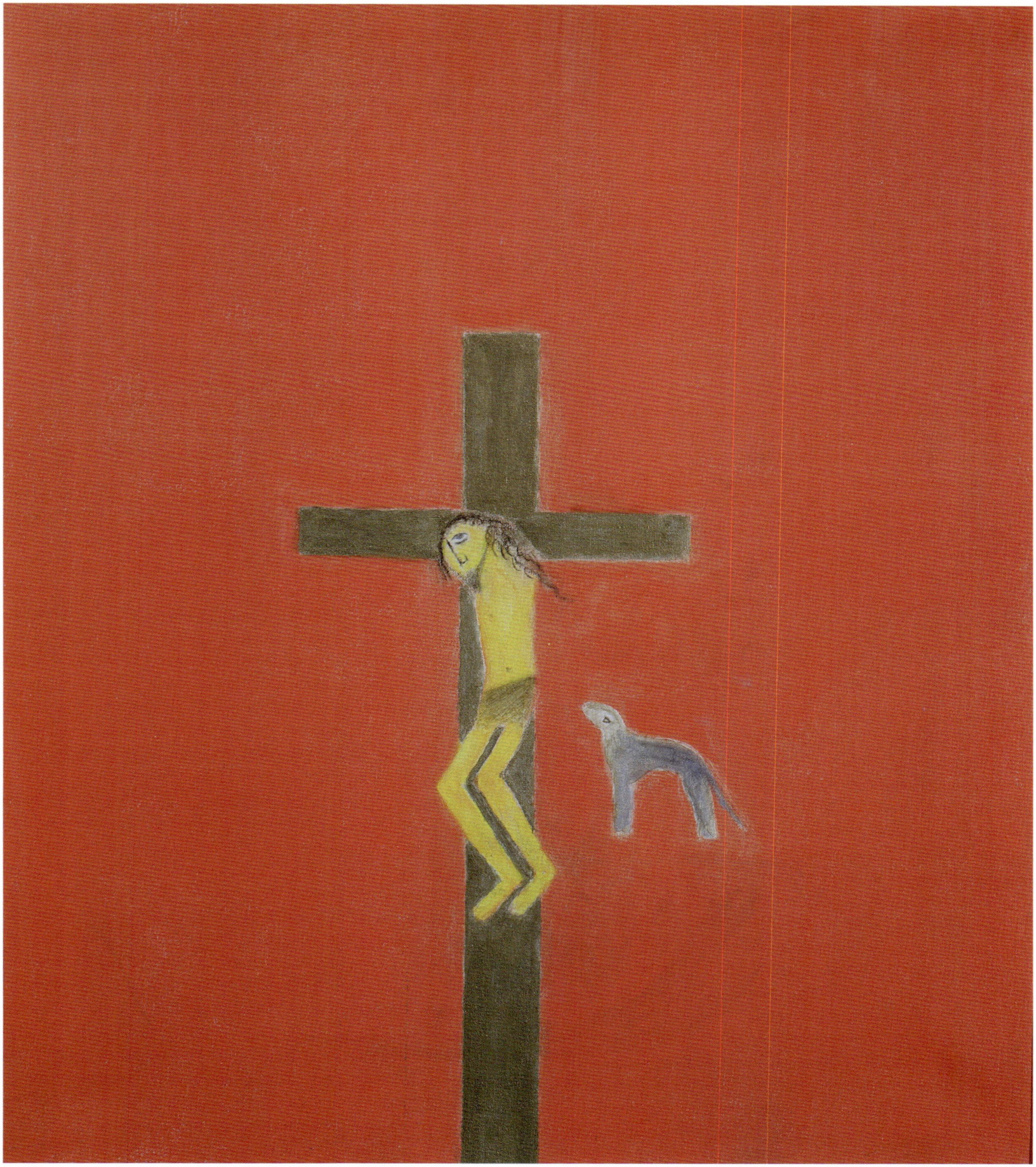

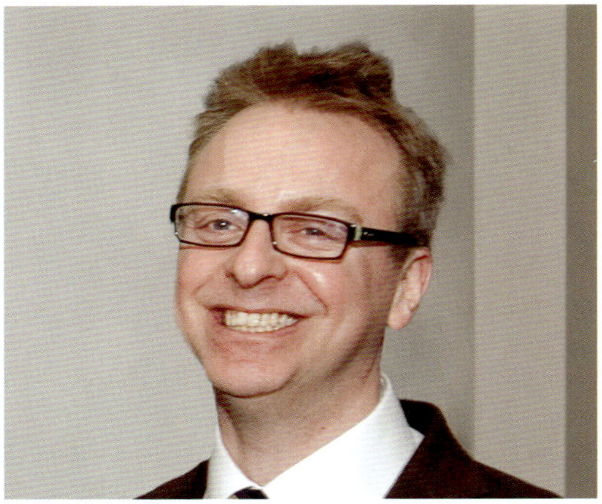

Philip Long has co-written a number highly praised publications to accompany exhibitions at the Dean Gallery and Scottish National Gallery of Modern Art, including *Scottish Colourists 1900–1930*, (toured to Royal Academy of Arts, London, 2000), *Charles Rennie Mackintosh in France 1923–7* as well as catalogues on artists William Gillies, John Maxwell, Anne Redpath, Elizabeth Blackadder, John Houston and designer Basil Spence. Recently he has undertaken work on Artist Rooms, a collection of international contemporary art which has been collected by Anthony d'Offay. He is a member of the Heritage Lottery Committee for the Scottish Arts Council.

BAY AFTER STORM

JOHN HOUSTON OBE RSA RSW RGI (1930–2008)

1989–90, oil on canvas, 121.9x121.9 cm

Purchased 1990

The following is a quotation from *John Houston*, Philip Long, Scottish National Gallery of Modern Art, 2005 (exhibition catalogue)

'...John Houston does not base his work only on his observation of nature. During the process of their making, his paintings take on an independent life. This comes about as a result of the artist's intuitive response as to how a picture should develop once it is underway, most particularly at a point when, in his opinion, the work appears to have become too planned. Houston describes this work as 'losing his temper' with the picture and he relies on the energy this creates to help him bring back something of the mood which he first experienced in front of his chosen motif. The retention of that original feeling is constantly striven for above any truthful likeness to the subject, and he freely changes his composition to help him achieve this.'

– Chosen by Philip Long, Senior Curator, Scottish National Gallery of Modern Art.

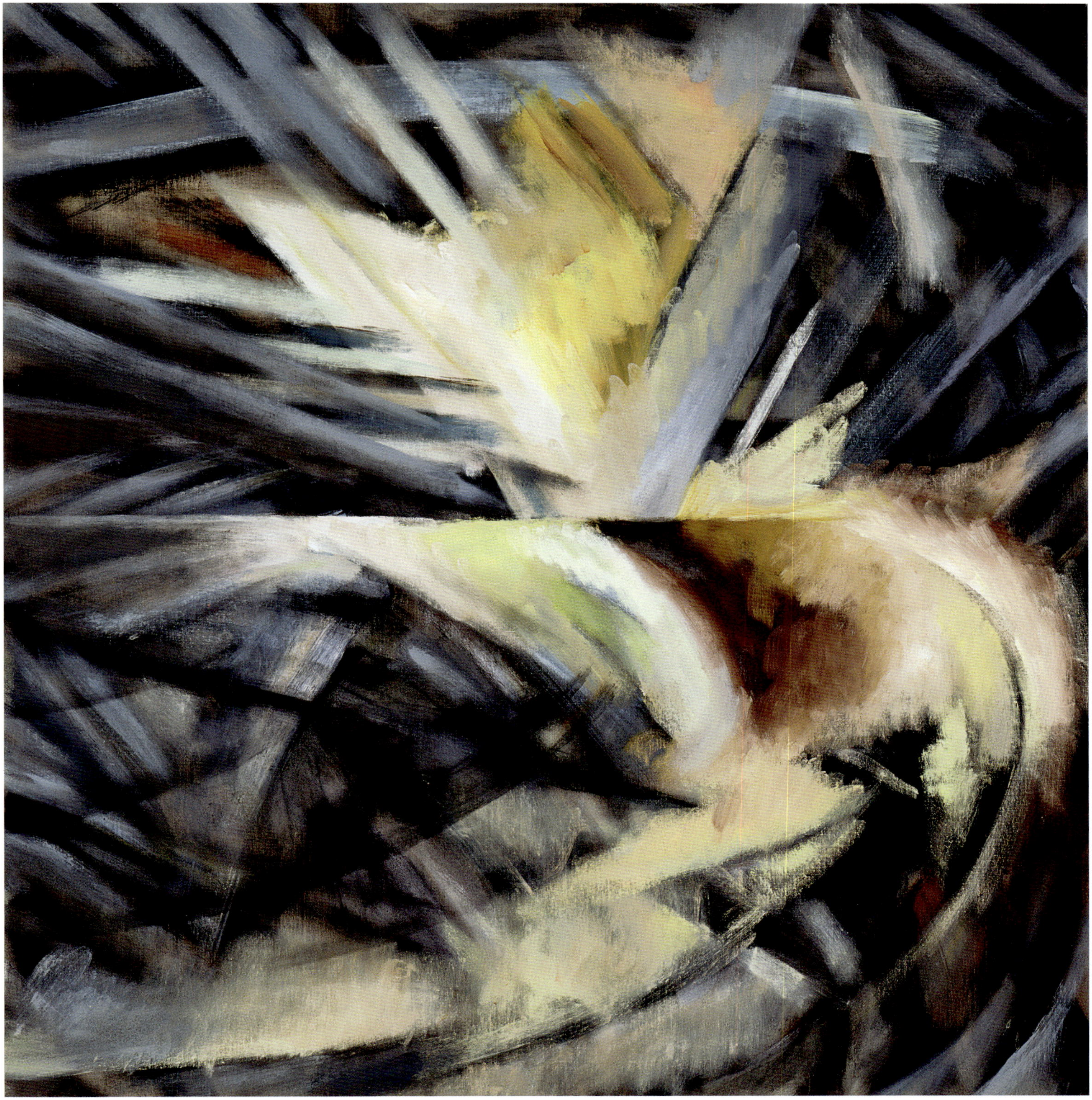

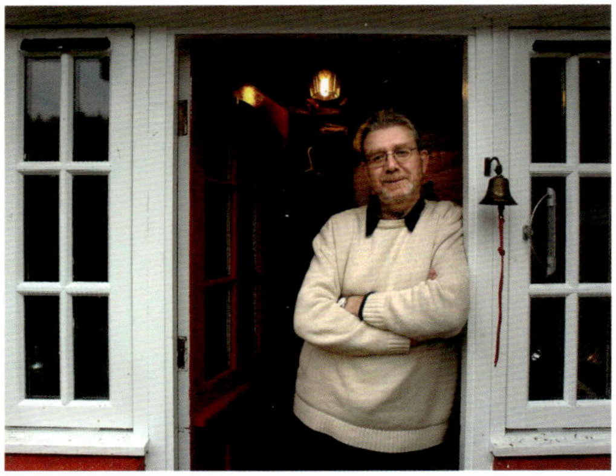

Michael Russell was born in Bromley, Kent and raised in his father's hometown of Troon, Ayrshire. He is the author of seven books, including a novel, and was a film director and newspaper culture columnist. First elected an MSP for the Scottish National Party in 1999 he became Scotland's Environment Minister in 2007. Since late 2009 he has served as Cabinet Secretary for Education and Lifelong Learning.

NORTH WEST PASSAGE, ARCTIC ROUTE

WILL MACLEAN RSA (b.1941)

1994, mixed media construction, 73x101 cm

Purchased 1995

'Mixed media fascinate me – so do artefacts that speak of the sea. Add in the uniquely Highland vision of Will Maclean and there was little doubt about what I would choose. In this work Maclean uses shapes, texture and faded colour – as well as a range of chosen and accidental materials – to speak of wind, water, ice and the exhausted lonely lives and deaths of so many who dared to explore; or who were forced to do so by privation at home. It is, like the best mixed media works, so much more than the sum of its parts. It makes me feel the weather on my face and the harsh reality of my rural inheritance.'

– Chosen by Michael Russell MSP, then Scotland's Minister for Culture, External Affairs and the Constitution.

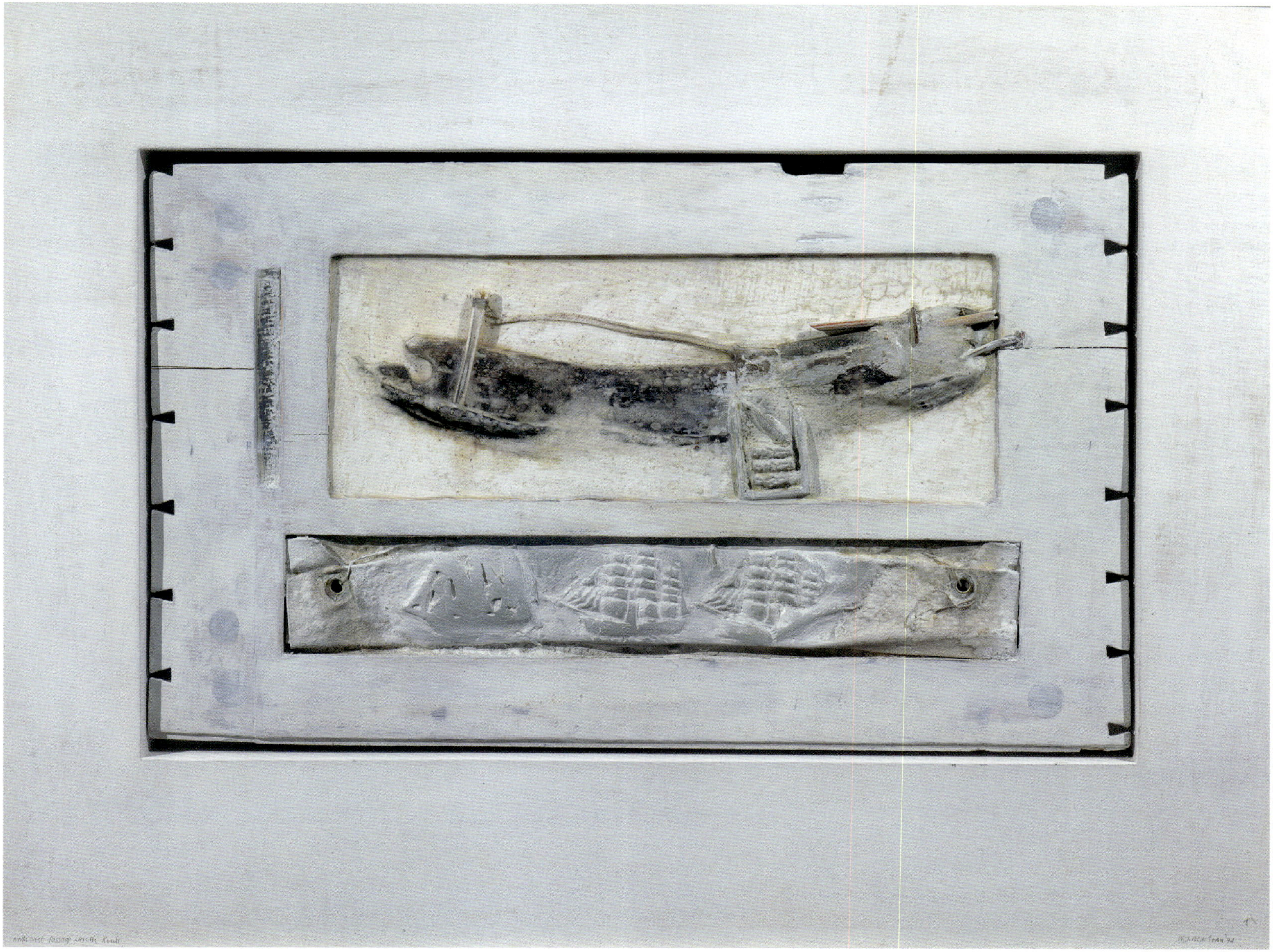

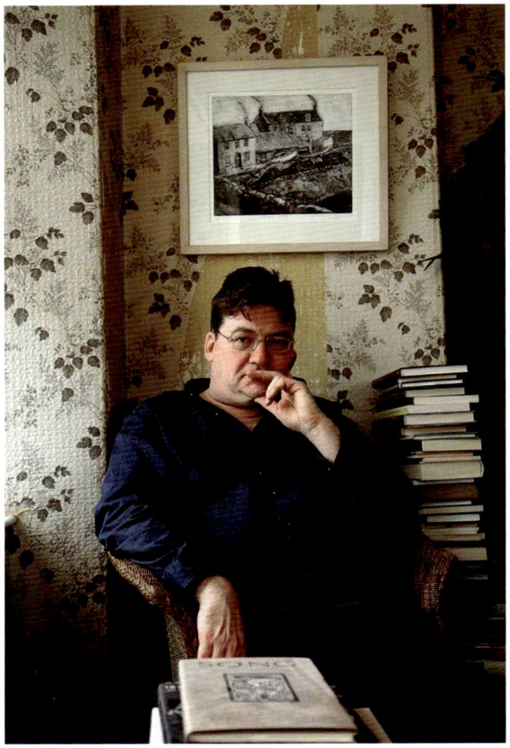

John Burnside, a former computer software engineer, is one of Scotland's best-loved poets. A winner of the Whitbread prize for poetry, he is also the author of several novels, whose short stories have been published in the New Yorker magazine. His memoir, *A Lie About My Father,* was published in 2006. He teaches at The University of St Andrews.

NORTH WEST PASSAGE, ARCTIC ROUTE

(Detail)

WILL MACLEAN RSA (b.1941)

1994, mixed media construction, 73x101 cm

Purchased 1995

'What I love here is the suggestion of a narrative that I cannot quite access, a world glimpsed through fog or tidal water, a lyrical history that – in some time of dreaming, some beyond – weaves land and weather and human making into a single fabric. This work reminds us of how the North West Passage – a practical, almost mercantile concept at the outset, a way of travelling more efficiently from A to B – was rendered mythical by epic loss and hope against hope, Franklin's party glimmering away in a blizzard like a faraway signal, their boats ruined, their souls blown to infinity.

There is no exaggeration here, no melodrama – and this is how myth works: it distils; it perfects; it tells us what we never expected to hear, yet knew all along. A true account that the mere facts could never render: stubborn; unjustified; beyond belief or doubt.'

– Chosen by John Burnside, Novelist and Poet.

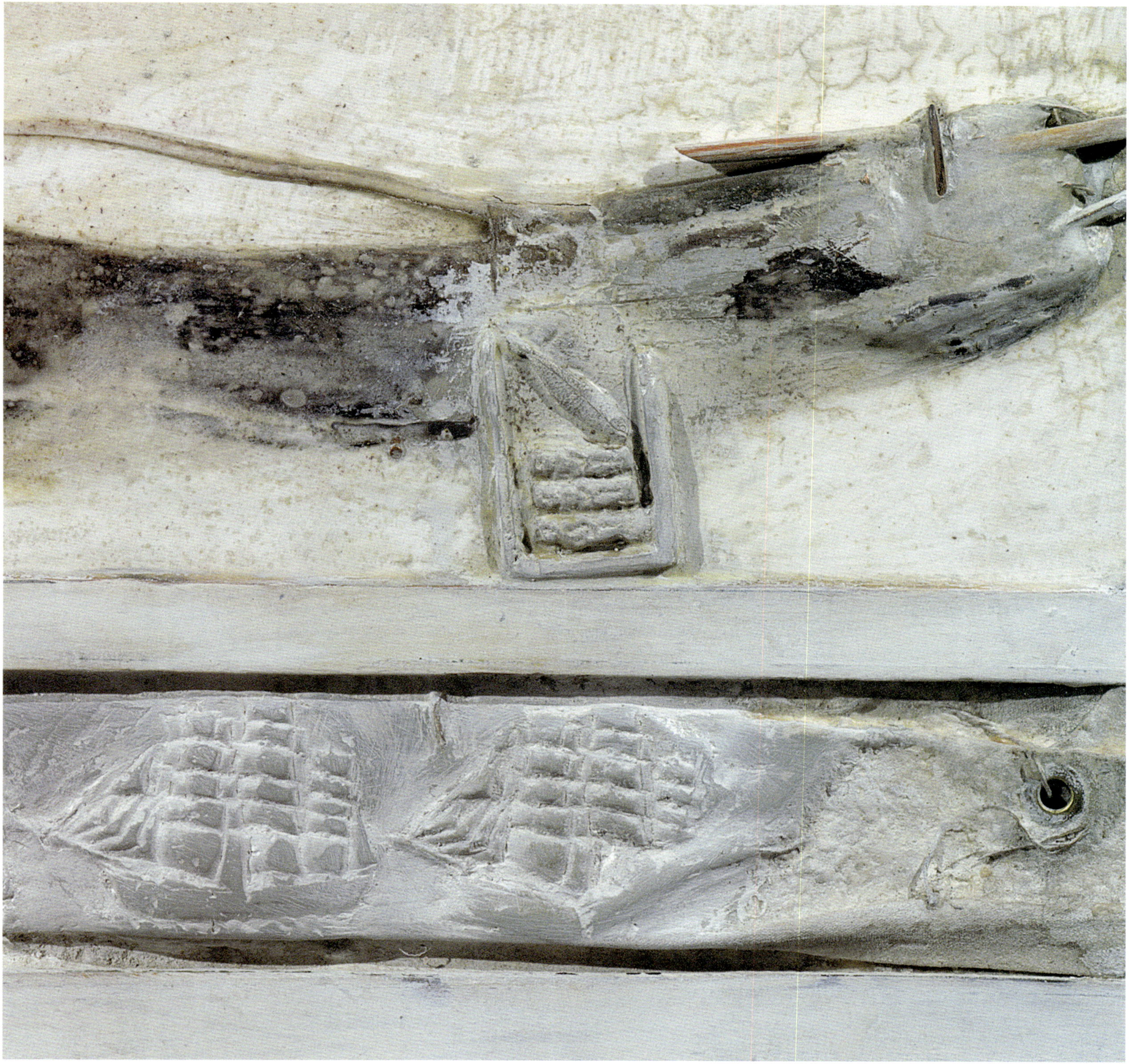

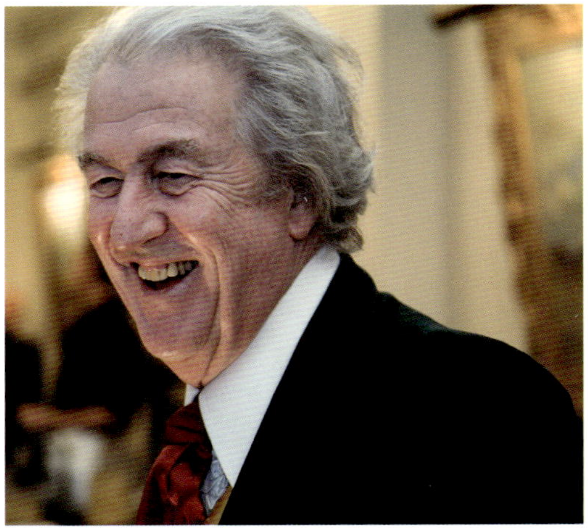

Allan Murray has long had a passion for Scottish Art, and this he shares with wife Carol, who is a fifth-generation Hong Kong Belonger. Scots-born Murray is a dedicated Clubman, and an indefatigable luncher at The Hong Kong Club, where over half the Murrays' extensive collection is on long-term loan. In the unending quest for 'large flat wall space' outwith their apartment, other works reside with The Heritage Trust for the North West (of England), the Kelvingrove Gallery, The National Trust for Scotland, and The National Galleries of Scotland, of which they are enthusiastic Sponsors. As an extension of his long career with Merchant Bankers, Jardine Fleming, he is now Chairman, Hong Kong Equity Broking for the successor company, JP Morgan Securities (Asia Pacific) Limited, and, to wit, is a Patron and Trustee of The Fleming-Wyfold Art Foundation, whose collection was a major early influence, when housed in the offices of Robert Fleming in London.

THE ETTRICK SHEPHERD

JOHN BELLANY CBE RA HRSA (b.1942)

1967, oil on canvas, 154.9x151.1 cm

Purchased 1987

'Witness the gaunt, weathered face of the shepherd, the unshorn coats of the sheep, the overshadowing emptiness of the hills, and the sheer simplicity of the composition, which is on a grand scale...

All conspire brilliantly to convey the harsh, lonely existence of a Borders 'hirt', and the bleakness of yon grim, dark expanse of emptiness that is the Southern uplands, where the drear of winter has been enlivened by an inspired dash of colour in the foreground.'

– Chosen by Allan G. Murray, Stockbroker and Trustee of The Fleming-Wyfold Art Foundation.

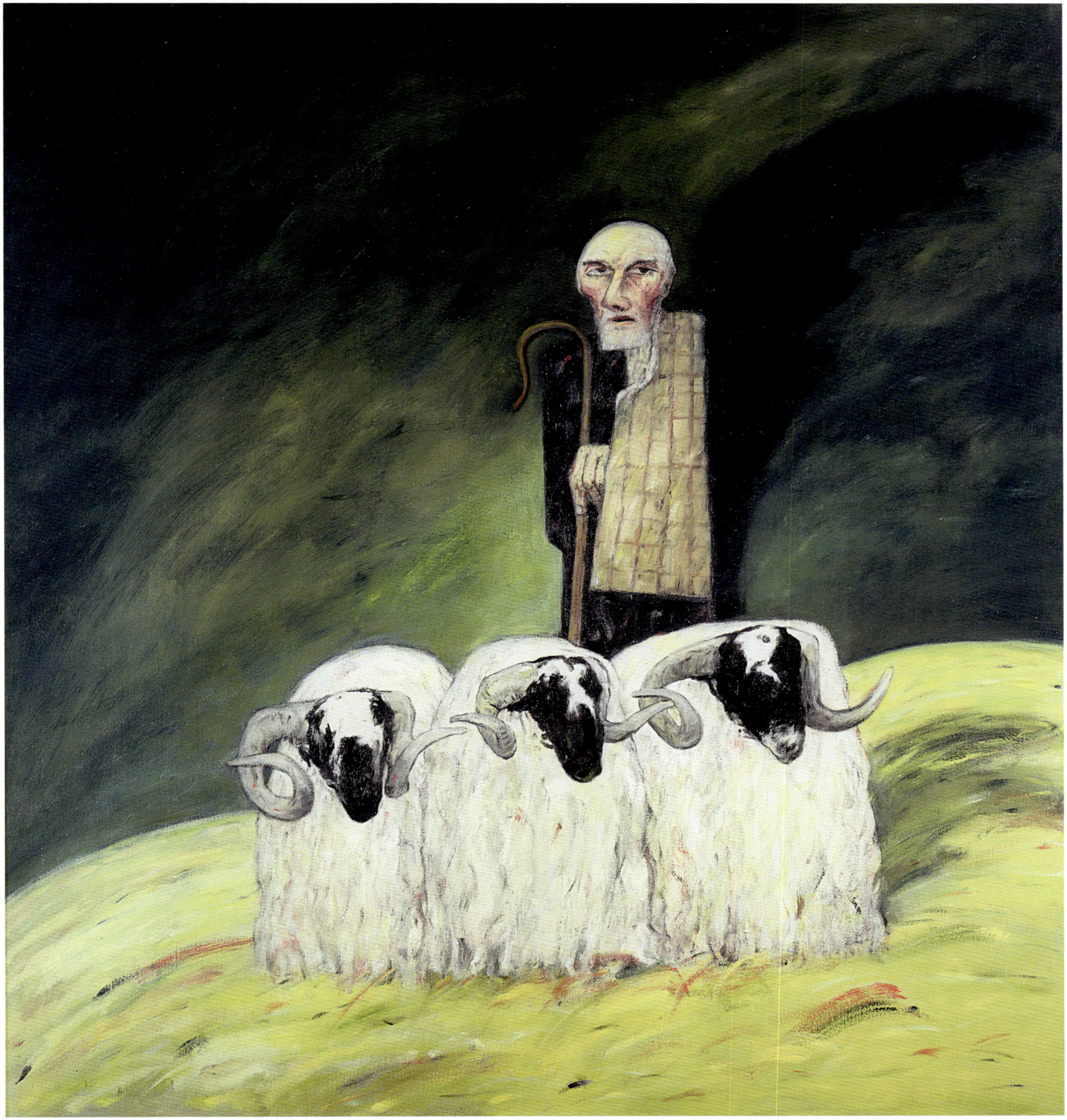

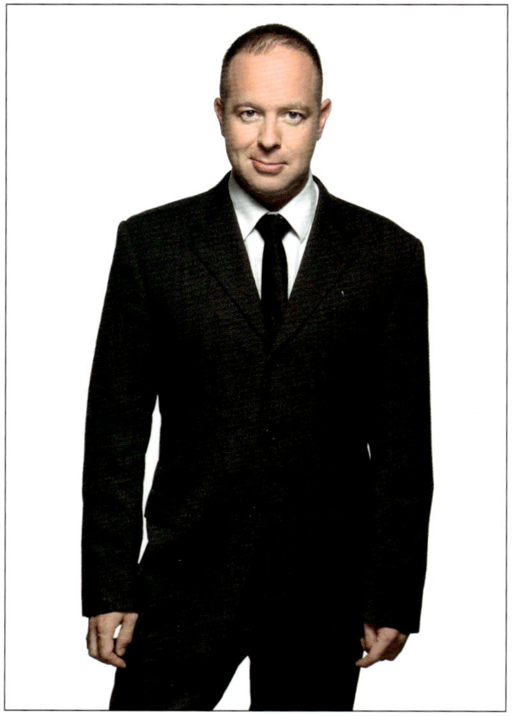

John Tiffany directed *Black Watch*, the National Theatre of Scotland play about soldiers of the Scottish Regiment and their service in Iraq, which won four Oliver awards in 2009, including best director for John Tiffany. He is Associate Director for new work at the National Theatre of Scotland and previous successes include *The Straits* for the London's Paines Plough company and *Gagarin's Way*.

WHERE ONCE THERE WERE SHIPS (CLYDE STREET, BROOMIELAW, GLASGOW)

GARY ANDERSON (b.1960)

2000, watercolour and crayon on paper, 71.1x53.3 cm

Purchased 2000

'I find Anderson's painting incredibly evocative of the city I've adopted as my hometown. It's murky and mysterious; it lures me in despite initial trepidation. It suggests one reality, but conceals another that is entirely different.

This is an astoundingly well-crafted painting. Characters and stories abound, whispering histories from shadowy nooks. Life thrives as mould and grasses and a vast blue sky reaches upwards into an optimistic future.

There's real drama in this other story: the story of this surprising, resilient Glasgow character, pushing forward but honour-bound and ever-indebted to the ship builders who made her great.'

– Chosen by John Tiffany, Theatre Director.

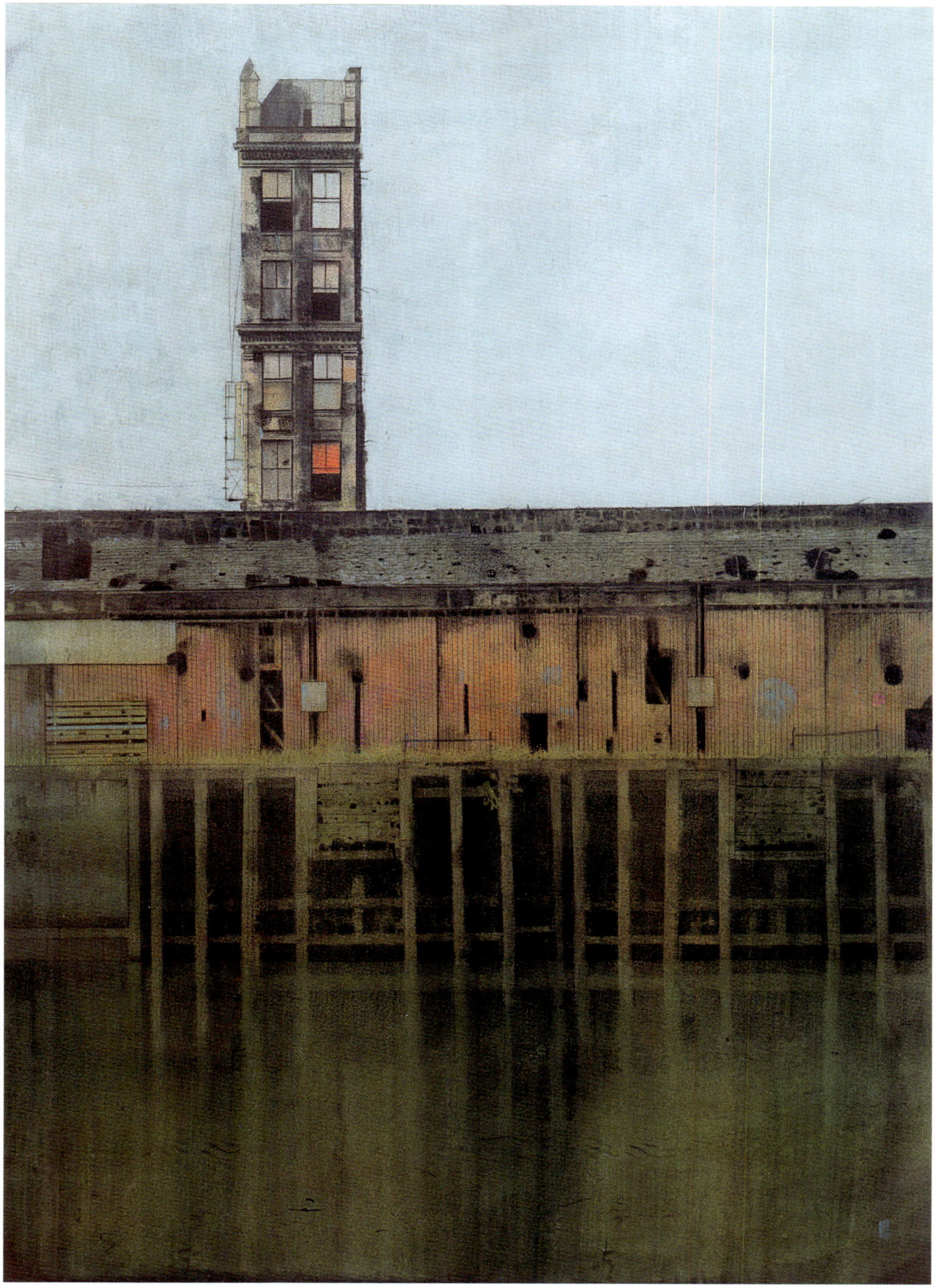

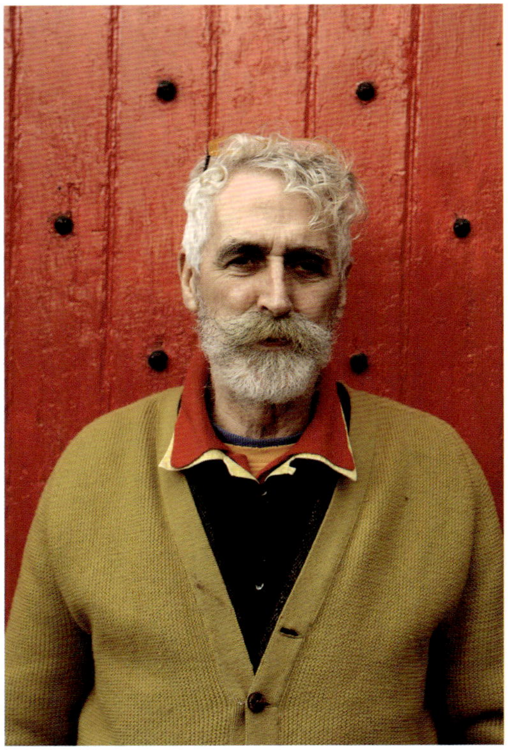

John Byrne was born in Barshaw, Paisley. He worked as a "slab boy" in A.F. Stoddart's carpet factory before enrolling in 1958 at Glasgow School of Art. He worked as a graphic designer for Scottish television. Byrne's interest in film and popular culture took off in earnest when he started working on an animated film with the singer Donavon in 1970. He began designing theatre sets for a wide variety of productions including Billy Connolly's *The Great Northern Welly Show*. He also designed a number of album covers and painted the Beatles for the *Illustrated Beatles Lyrics*. Byrne's prodigious talent as a painter is sometimes overshadowed by the immense success for his work for stage and screen, including *The Slab Boys* and *Tutti Frutti*. In 2000 Paisley Museum and Art Galleries marked Byrne's sixtieth birthday with a retrospective exhibition.

RIVER THE COLOUR OF LEAD

PETER THOMPSON (b.1962)

2007, acrylic on panel, 40x65cm

Purchased 2007

'This picture is quite surprising and quite monumental in the sweep of the landscape, in a very, very individual style. It reminded me of American early twentieth-century folk paintings; it doesn't fit into any Scottish school that I can think of. I like the positioning of it as well, lots of sticky up trees in a barren landscape. There is a sense of desolation about it, but not in a contrived way, not something that gets you down at all. A very acute eye. He picked a fine part of the country.

I really loved the detail of it. To talk about technique is bye the bye, but it's as far as you can get from photography, which is wonderful, and it's a very complete image. There's a bleak poetry about it, but it has a grandeur of scale. Personally I don't do landscape at all. I do landscape in backgrounds to portraits, but I don't do landscapes per se. I'll have figures in the foreground. I usually find landscapes very boring. Industrial landscapes I like very much, but you take a beauty spot somewhere, it would bore me to tears.'

– Chosen by John Byrne, Artist, Designer, Director, Playwright, Writer.

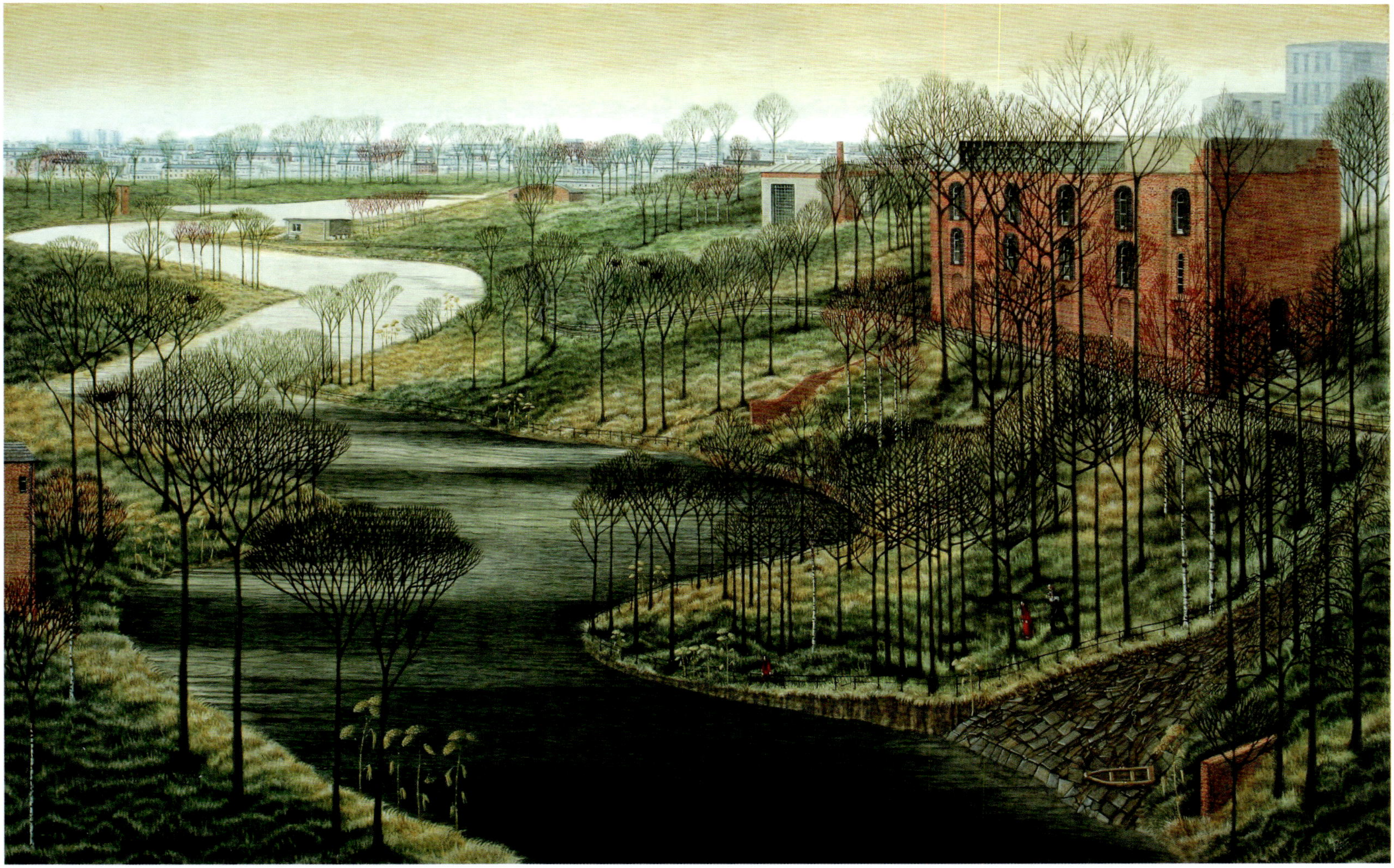

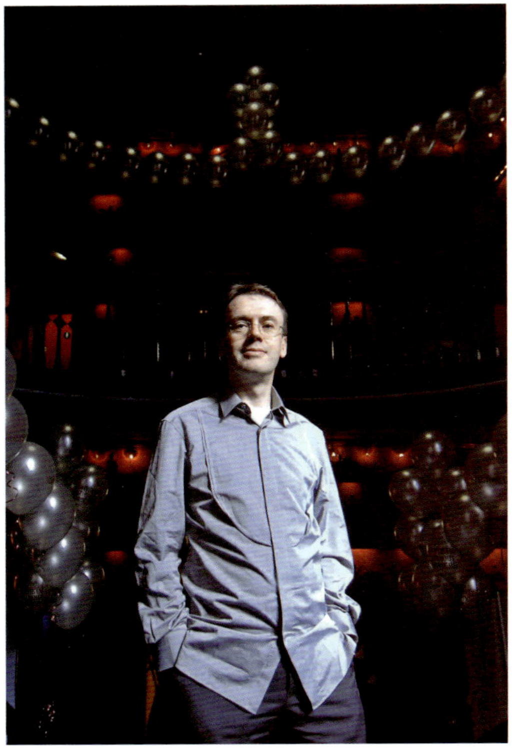

Jonathon Mills, an Australian academic and composer of contemporary opera was relatively unknown in Scotland until he was picked as Director of the Edinburgh International Festival in 2006. His line-up in 2009, from Faust to the music of the Enlightenment in Handel operas and Bach cantatas, was rated his strongest yet.

LABEL QUEEN OF HUNGARY

DERRICK GUILD (b.1963)

1996–7, oil on canvas, 81.3x69.9 cm

Purchased 1997

'I find myself immediately drawn to the historic figure seemingly trapped behind what appears at once to be iron bars yet, on closer inspection, is depicted on a grid of swing-tags – the type used equally for labeling consumer goods in shops or identifying works in museum storage or display.

Only one of the twenty-four 'labels' suggests that we are looking at an individual rather than a figurehead – and even the facial features depicted are fairly generic. Clearly the painter has cast the subject as an historic figure – her appearance and regalia, the lace collar, the period hairstyle and stylised features – yet she is not depicted as one would expect a Royal to be – included are modest jewellery and what appear to be simple fabrics.

It is the combination of this uncertainty in the context of a traditional medium – oil painting – with a familiar subject – an historic portrait – that provides the intrigue which sustains the viewer's attention; literally someone whose identity is inextricably linked with the labels that have been applied to them; someone, therefore, with whom we can all relate.'

– Chosen by Jonathan Mills, Festival Director, Edinburgh International Festival.

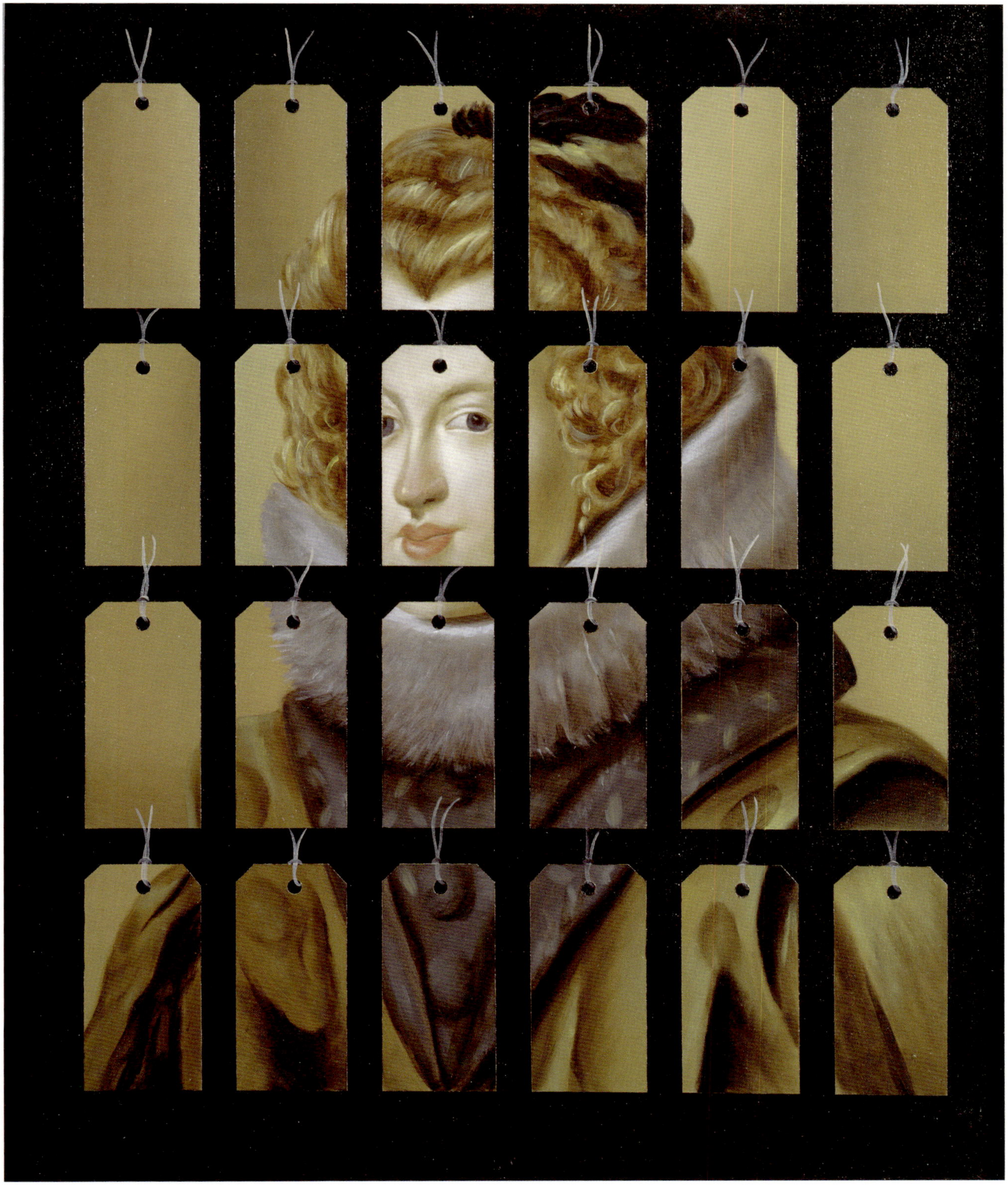

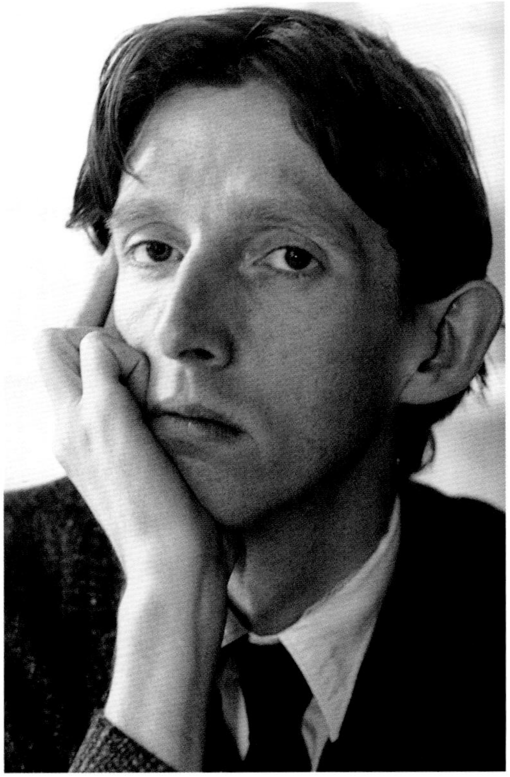

Matthew Sturgis read History at Oxford, worked for four years in publishing, and since then has made his living as a freelance writer and critic. He has written art criticism for Harpers & Queen, travel pieces for the Sunday Telegraph and football reports for the Independent on Sunday amongst many other subjects. His cartoons have been published in the Oldie and the Daily Mail. His books include *Passionate Attitudes: The English Decadence of the 1890s* published in 1995 by Macmillan and the highly-praised biographies of Aubrey Beardsley and Walter Sickert. He is married to the gallery owner Rebecca Hossack, and lives in London.

CANUTE

HELEN FLOCKHART (b.1963)

1997, oil on canvas, 114.3x144.8 cm

Purchased 1997

'The mediaeval chronicler Henry of Huntingdon provides the earliest record of King Canute's memorable encounter with the waves. The act, it seems, was not motivated by royal pride, but by a sense of Christian humility. As Canute sat enthroned on the seashore, the incoming tide washing over his feet, he proclaimed to his courtiers the limits of temporal kingship, and the true greatness of God – who alone could command the waters.

Helen Flockhart's luminous painting is clearly not a mere illustration of Henry of Huntingdon's chronicle. It is something more. Her red-haired king is alone, no shore in sight, the green waves rising towards his chest. He seems locked in a solitary contest or dialogue with the deep. With brow set, he leans into the swell, perhaps striving against the tide, or perhaps seeking to become part of it.

The meticulous details, the exquisite craftsmanship, the gem-like quality of the light, all add to the concentrated energy of the image. There is a sense of yearning and pathos: of Man's desire to become, once again, subsumed into the wholeness of Nature.'

– Chosen by Matthew Sturgis, Historian, Biographer.

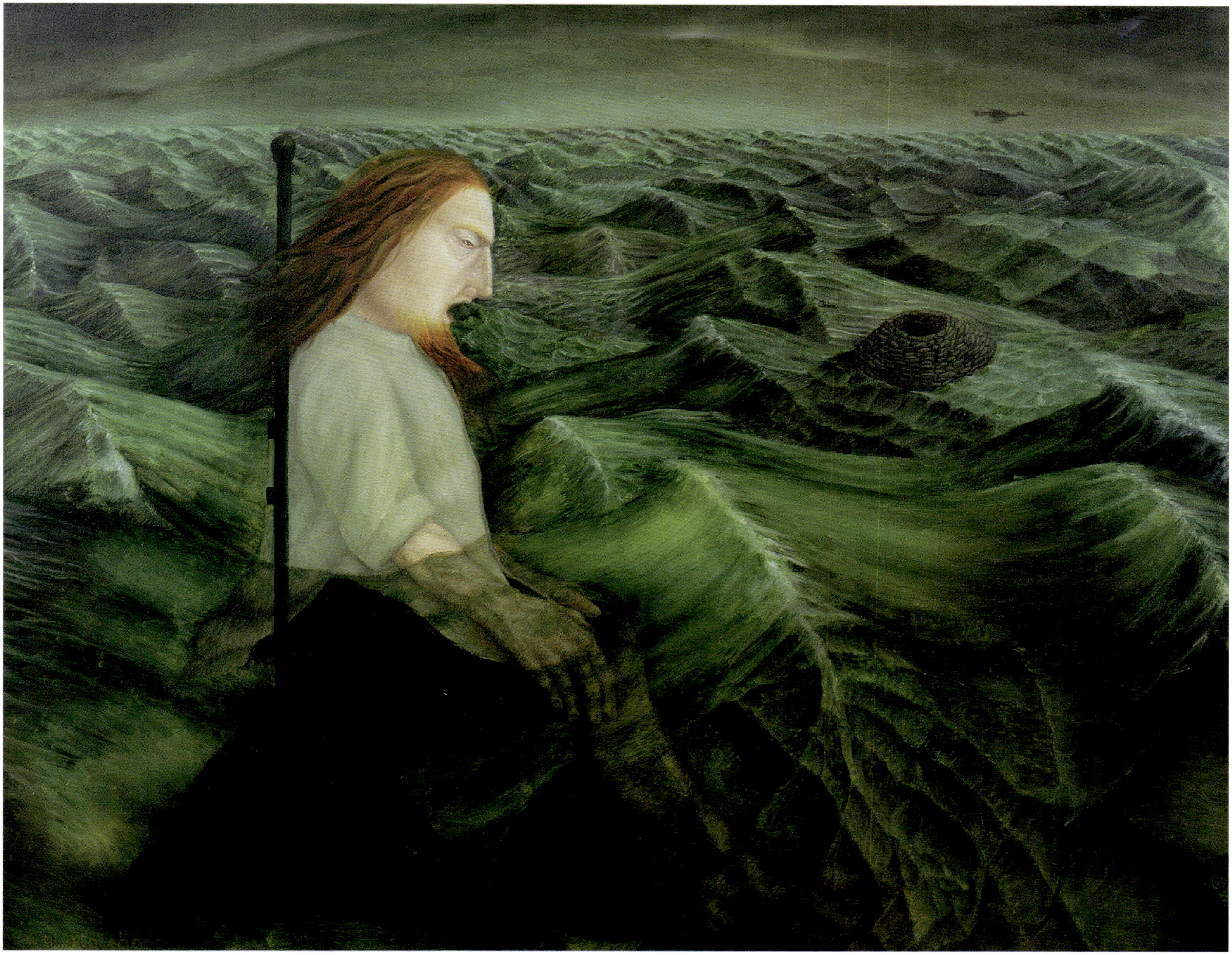

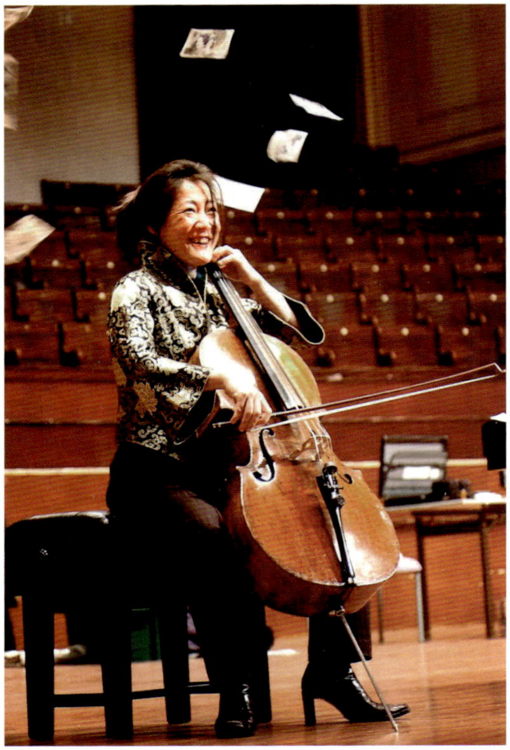

Su-a Lee was born in Seoul, Korea and won a scholarship to Chetham's School of Music in Manchester, aged nine. She subsequently studied at the Juilliard School in New York. She has been with the Scottish Chamber Orchestra for nearly ten years and is a dynamic presence on the Scottish classical and contemporary scene. She is a founder member of the Mr McFall's Chamber, a string quartet first launched to introduce classical music to non-classical listeners by taking contemporary music to the late night club circuit. As a consequence of Su-a's selection of Alan Kilpatrick's work, they met and subsequently devised a musical and artistic collaboration, *Tipping the Scales of Justice*, which was first performed at The Fleming Collection in 2009 and has led to other joint projects.

WHERE THE BRAHAMPUTRA MEETS THE CLYDE SERIES

ALAN KILPATRICK (b.1963)

2003, charcoal and graphite on paper, 29x20 cm

Purchased 2004

'As a person who revels in colour and delights in exuberance, I was delighted to find that I was immediately drawn to Alan Kilpatrick's charcoal and graphite series *Where the Brahamaputra Meets the Clyde*.

Perhaps it is the pure beauty and serenity of the scenes. Perhaps it is the stimulation given here for contemplating these two great rivers on opposite sides of the world; the realisation that all waters of the world are inevitably connected. Or perhaps it is also that I have visited India a few times, where the contrasts within the country are so striking on every level.

These images represent for me an organic integration of two essentially disparate nations.'

– Chosen by Su-a Lee, Sub-Principal Cellist, Scottish Chamber Orchestra.

Images: Opposite, clockwise from top:
Where the Brahamputra meets the Clyde No. 3, Where the Brahamputra meets the Clyde No. 5, Where the Brahamputra meets the Clyde No. 11, Where the Brahamputra meets the Clyde No. 10

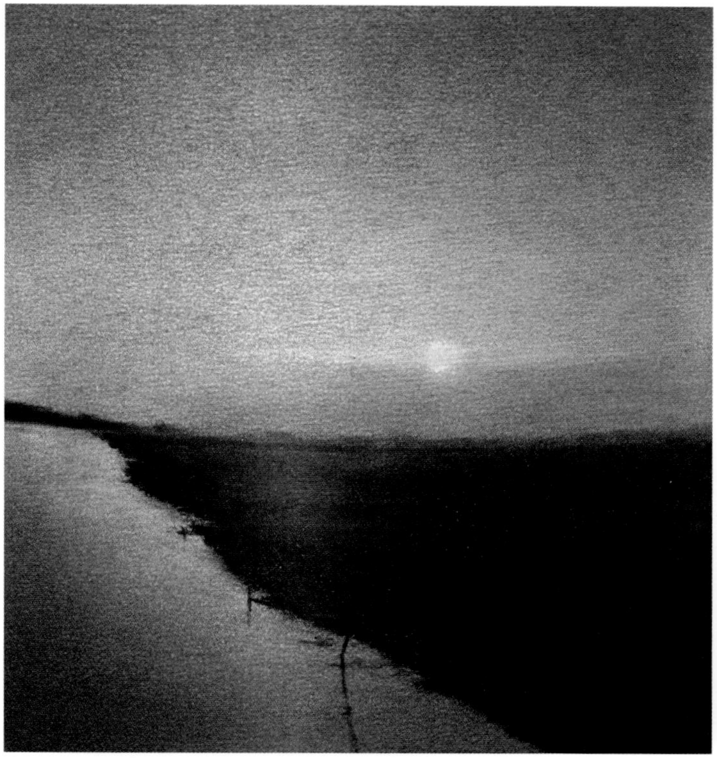
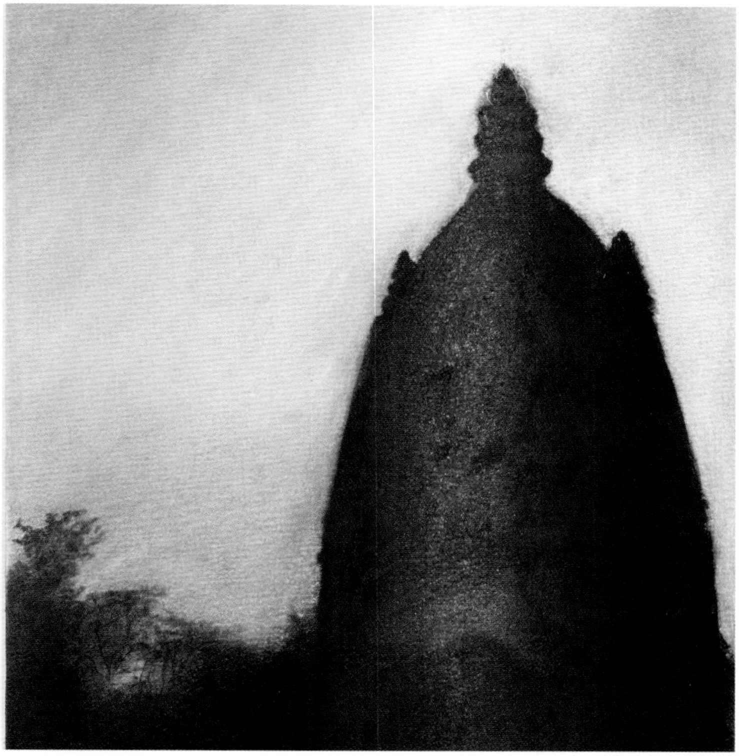
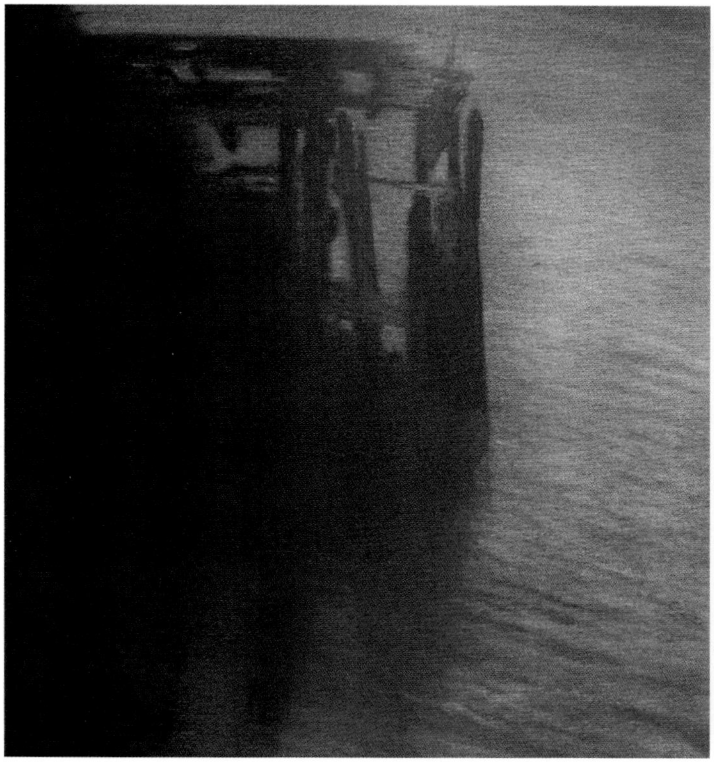
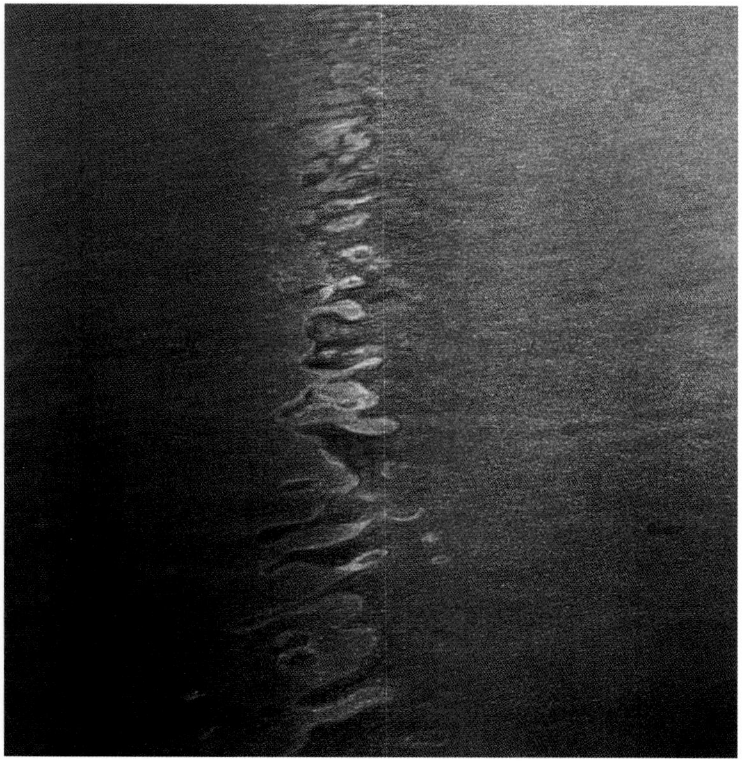

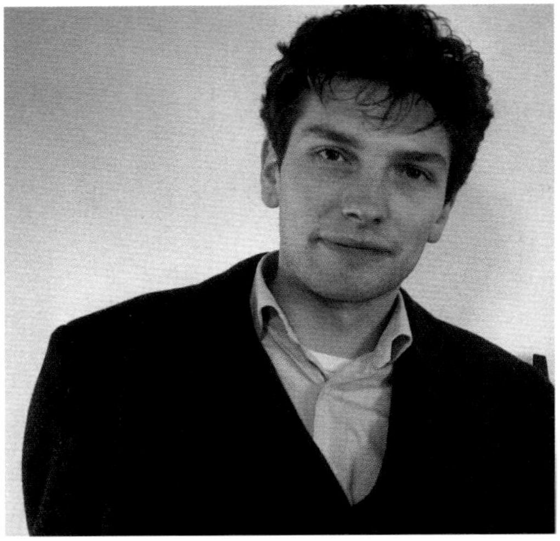

Andrew Macdonald was born in Glasgow and is the grandson of the Hungarian emigre screenwriter-director Emeric Pressburger. He is well known for his collaborations with screenwriter John Hodge and director Danny Boyle, including *Shallow Grave* (1994), *Trainspotting* (1996) and *A Life Less Ordinary* (1997). Together with Duncan Kenworthy, he is also the founder of DNA Films, the production company responsible for *The Parole Officer* (2001), *28 Days Later* (2002), *Sunshine* (2007) and *Last King of Scotland* (2006), two of which Danny Boyle directed and Alex Garland wrote.

WIRELESS VISION ACCOMPLISHED

STEPHEN CONROY (b.1964)

1987, oil on canvas, 137.1x121.9 cm

Purchased 1988

'Stephen Conroy comes from Dumbarton near where I grew up. He did me a huge favour to lend four of his paintings for *Shallow Grave,* a film I produced in Glasgow. There is a great scene in the film between Kerry Fox and Keith Allen that happens under Stephen's picture. The only cost was the insurance. I remember thinking how much I would love that painting... still would.'

– **Chosen by Andrew Macdonald, Film Producer.**

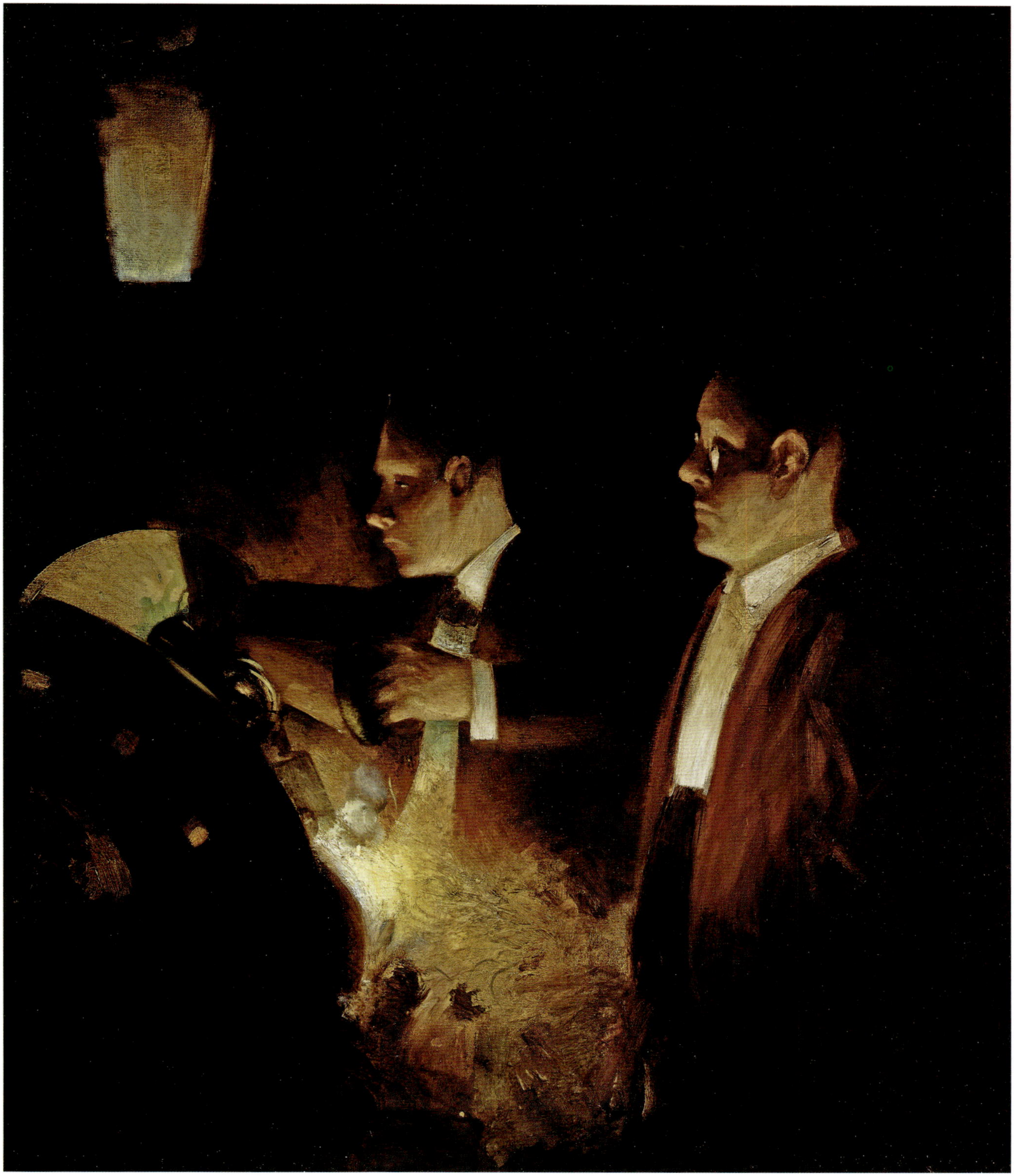

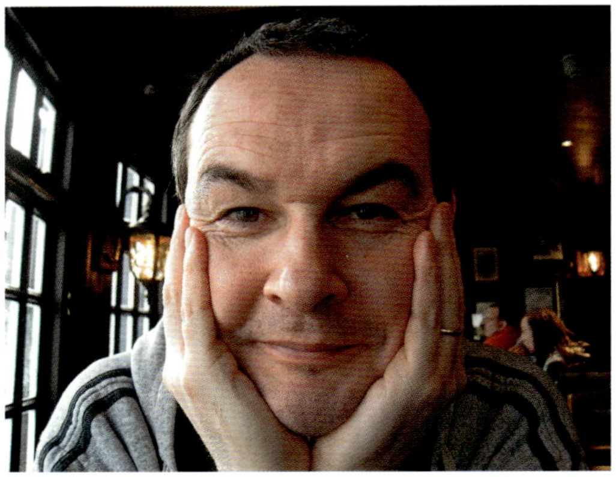

Chris Lee is an Irish writer living in London. His plays include *Hummingbird* at The Old Red Lion in 1996, *The Optimist's Daughters* at The Finborough in 1997 and *The Electrocution of Children* at The Abbey Theatre, Dublin, in 1998, for which he won The Stewart Parker Award. Chris was Anglo Irish Bank Writer in Association at The Abbey in 2000. Other plays include *The Map Maker's Sorrow* at The Abbey in 1999, *Eat the Enemy* at The Old Red Lion in 1999, *On Line and Paranoid* at The Finborough in 2000, *Vermilion Dream* at The Salisbury Playhouse in 2004 and *The Ash Boy* at Theatre 503 in 2006. His new play *The Water Harvest* opened at Theatre 503 in June 2009. His plays have also been performed in New York, Houston, Copenhagen and Paris.

THE PHILOSOPHER'S RIDGE

JANICE McNAB (b.1964)

2006, oil on board, 100x126 cm

Purchased 2006

'This painting inspired a short play performed by The Clamjamfry Company at The Fleming Collection in 2007. I love the cool grey and white colours of the painting and the mysterious figures on the mountain, which is of course a volcano.'

The following is a short extract from the play:

'Man: Stare into the belly of the earth. That is where fire was born and that is where fire hides. It is out of my reach. It taunts me. Do I have the courage to climb down inside the burning gut of this mountain and steal the flames? It may consume me. I lie here and in my mind I rip the heat from the liquid rock. I am a hero and I return to you with the gift of fire. I restore to you all the warmth that was taken from you. I am dreaming the mountain, and I am part of its dream.'

– Chosen by Chris Lee, Playwright.

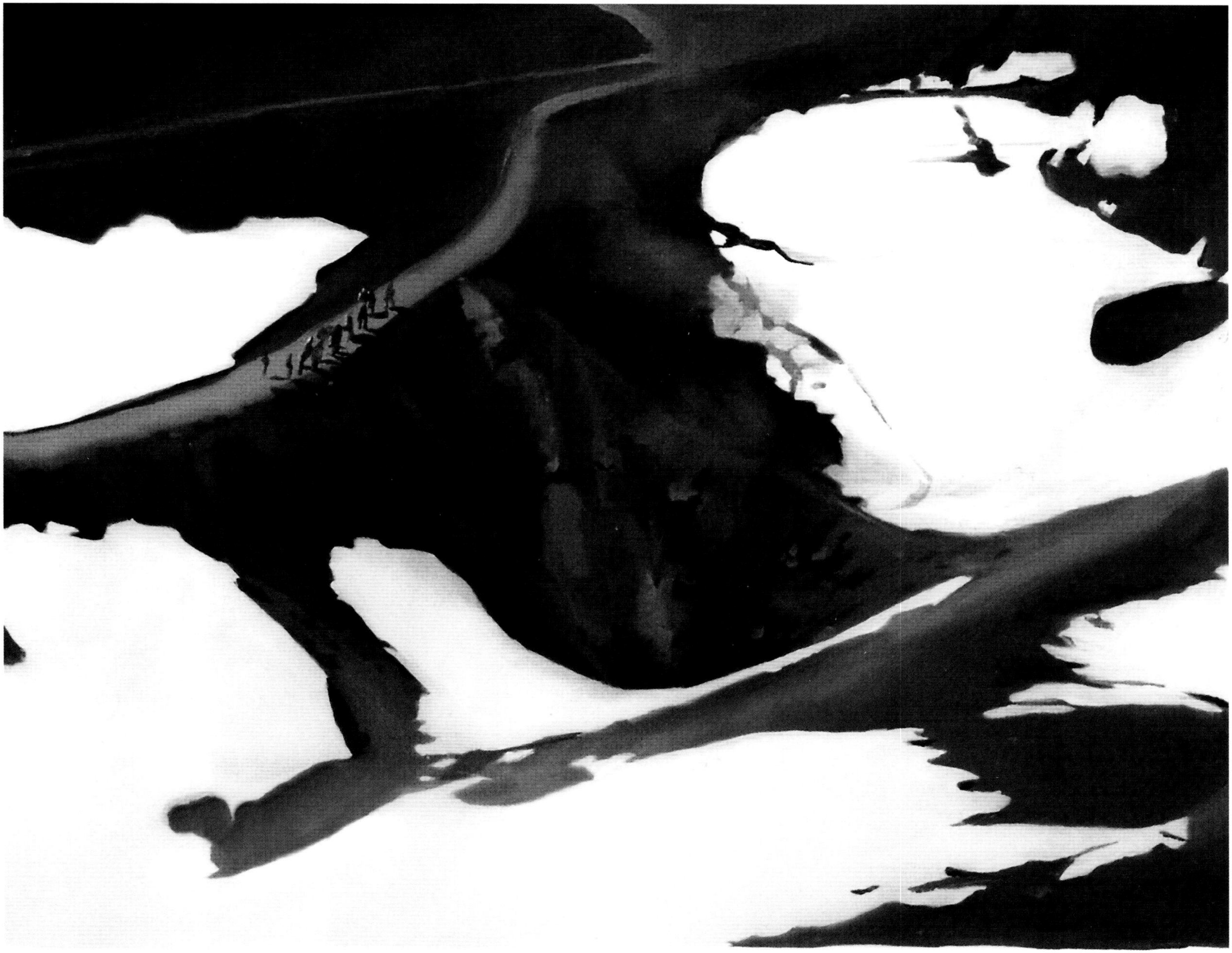

FLOCK OF BIRDS

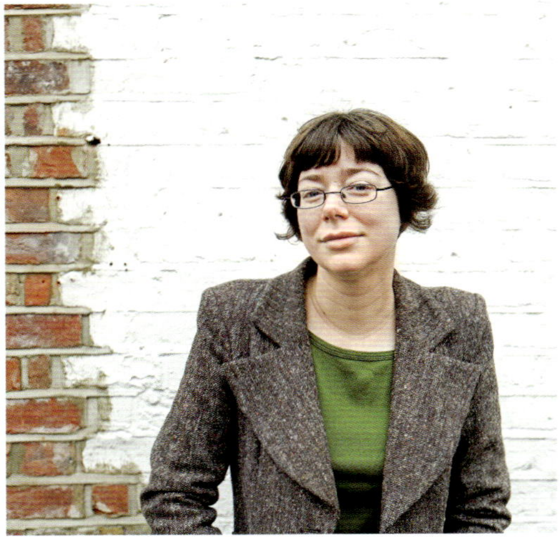

ALASDAIR WALLACE (b.1967)

1999, acrylic on canvas, 137.1x152.4 cm

Purchased 1999

– Chosen by Jen Hadfield, Writer.

Jen Hadfield was the winner of the TS Eliot Prize for poetry in 2008 for her collection of poetry *Nigh-No-Place,* which was written in Canada and Shetland. Hadfield lives in Shetland and its landscape and language persistently influence her poetry and visual art. Her work often pivots on the idea of the secular-sacred, relating to landscape – "it is in heaven as it is on earth" "it is on earth as it is in heaven." Liturgical rhythms underpin many of her poems about place, home, ecology, space – and idiomatic mythology of the here-and-now. Her book, *Almanacs* published by Bloodaxe, was written in Shetland and the Western Isles and won an Eric Gregory Award in 2003.

hung jury[1]

craff or spadger, binkie or chye, gyp or jacob – jeremy
joy – mock-a-pie, kya or jaikie – whelp or barker – waifchat, riphook,
purse-bill – pip, puck – parson or parish-duck – precinct myna – hoodie,
moonie, devil-squealer – come-in-along-us – little teacher – boatswain, riley,
– creepie, nine-killer – mollie-washdish, sea mouse, elsie worry – glue-throat,
smog-goose, olf or bully– scribbler, sombre – spoonbilled nurse-bird– noose
-gull, gawky or gog – blame-cuckoo: vagrant, royal, bluewing,baikal – crank,
yaffle – migrant or marching daw – goldie, gladdie – caudy maudy– little
drummer of the north – fool, flitterchack, five-amp – philip
flapper

[1] (the land a wiped slate, the licked plate of the air)

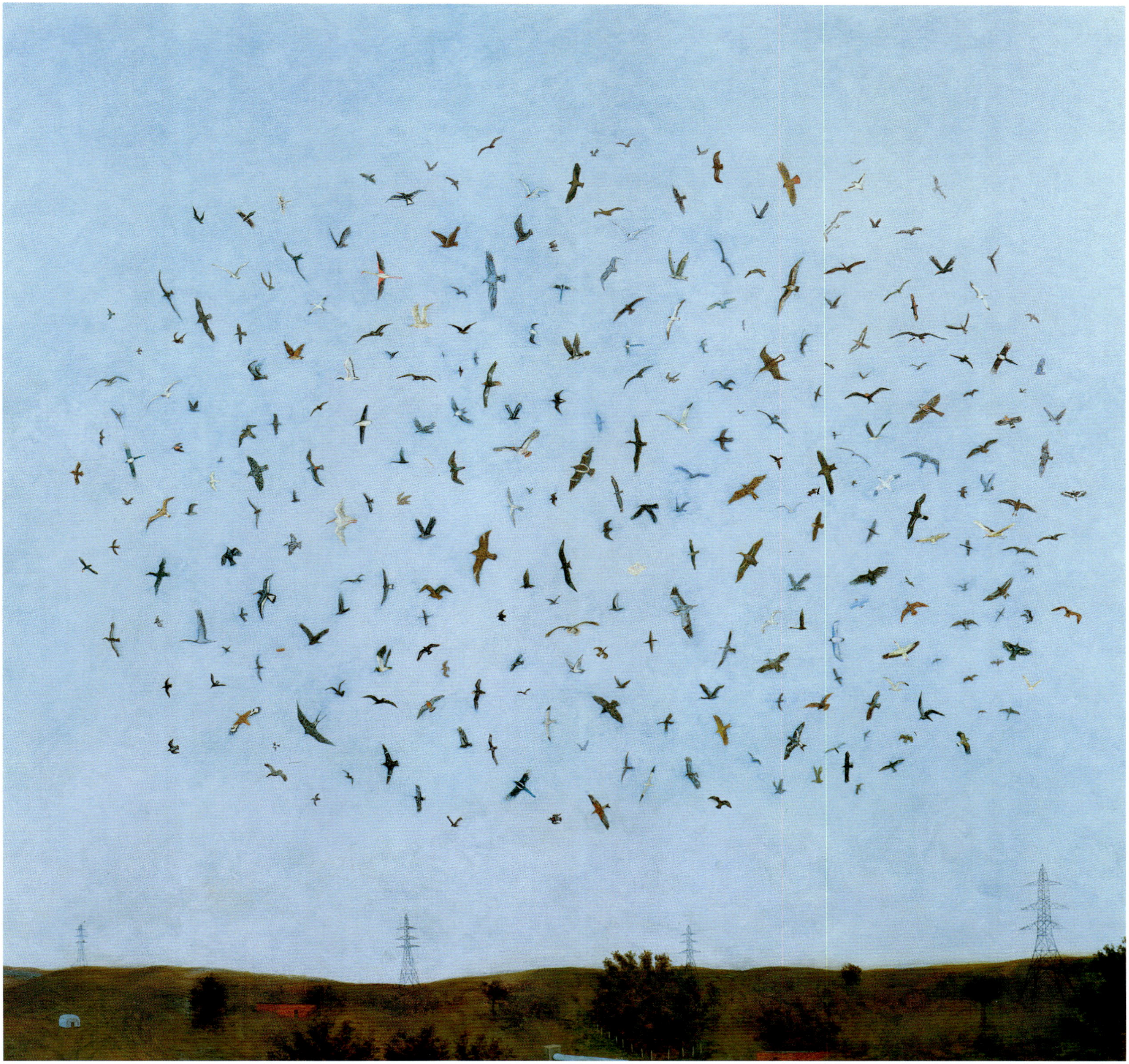

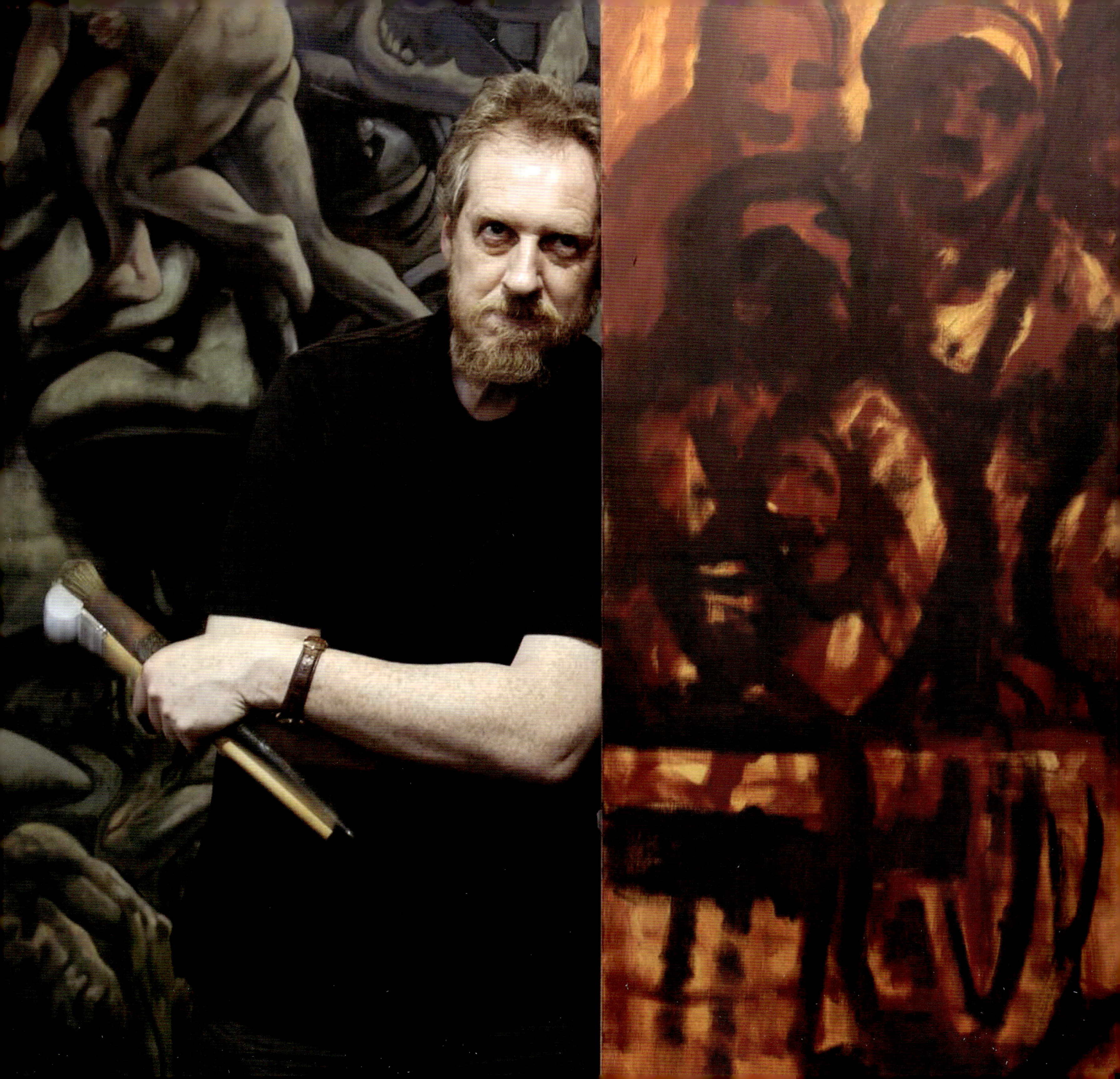

THE UNKNOWN CORNER

JAMES PRYDE (1866–1941)

1912, oil on canvas, 18.3x14.9 cm

Purchased 1988

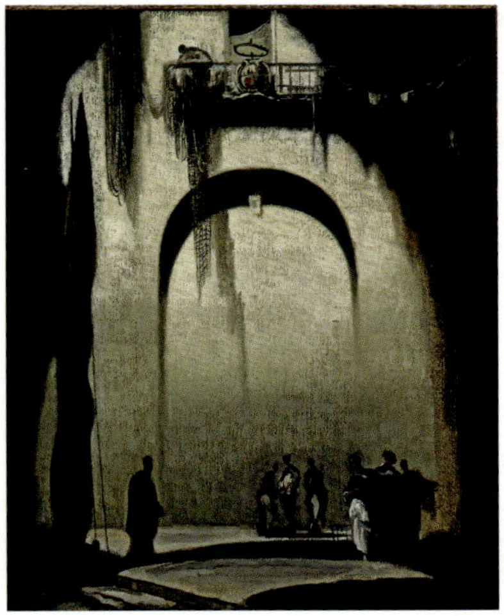

Peter Howson interviewed by Tim Cornwell, 23 March 2009

James Pryde is a particularly interesting artist, as a person, and a marvellous painter of atmosphere. He's a mixture of Daumier and Goya for me. In the paintings that he's most well-known for, there's a tremendous atmosphere. He works with a limited palette, doesn't use much colour, it's about tone and small patches of colour.

I don't know what this painting is about – I don't think anyone does. It's a romance, but the romance of darkness, there's no exuberance in these paintings. It certainly looks menacing, with that huge area of nothingness, and there is always something to catch your eye. It's almost as if a giant scythe is about to come down on these people, like death, it's a shadow on the wall caused by an alcove, but while the upturned horseshoe is a symbol of protection and hope, this goes down the way, to me it's a symbol of an evil presence.

Pryde was a bit of a strange character altogether, what attracts me to him is he was an alcoholic, myself being a recovering alcoholic; you remain an alcoholic to the end of your days, I've just stopped drinking. He was supposedly alcoholic, melancholic, and a Bohemian. If he died in poverty, he wasn't very good with money. I'm not very good with money. I can certainly understand the idea of letting go and leading a Bohemian lifestyle. Melancholy is what I suffer from regularly, between bouts of ecstasy.

The genius of the painting is the use of the spaces. There's one absolute touch of genius, almost in the middle of the painting, veering towards the west is the net that hangs over. It reminds me of Canaletto in the way he has done it, this one touch, this wee bit of net hanging down, it's almost like a spider's web over this scythe-shaped shadow. It has a touch of Goya's black paintings about it, the paintings Goya did at the very end of his life, a lot of small paintings of cannibalism and rapes and murders.

It's nearly all tonal apart from a few flashes of colour, there's only one area of the painting that's white, that's the woman's dress, most of the figures are in shadow, but there's one part of the bustle of the dress that is pure white. It catches your attention right away, your eye immediately goes to that area, because eighty per cent of the painting is a creamy colour that's almost a white. It's very subtle, very beautiful. I will be interested to find out what people think of it, but I love it.

Peter Howson was born in London and trained at Glasgow School of Art. In 1992 he was commissioned by the Imperial War Museum to record the conflict in the former Yugoslavia, an event which changed his perspective entirely. He is represented in numerous public collections.

ADDITIONAL PARTICIPANTS

Wilhelmina Barns-Graham (1912–2004)
Spanish Elegy 1997
Susanna Beaumont
Director, doggerfisher, Edinburgh

Dame Elizabeth Blackadder (b.1931)
Irises, Brown and Yellow
Ian Howard
Principal, Edinburgh College of Art

John Byrne (b.1940)
Scottish Boy on the Beach with Japanese Wonder Shell 1995
Lucia Lindsay
Assistant Keeper of Art, The Fleming Collection

F.C.B. Cadell (1883–1937)
The Feathered Hat
George Plumtree
Former Managing Director, Bonhams

Nathan Coley (b.1967)
Lamp of Sacrifice – 286 Places of Worship, Edinburgh 2004
Celia Davies
Head of Projects, Photoworks

Robert Colquhoun (1914–1962)
Head Study
John Burningham
Artist, Illustrator, Author

Stephen Conroy (b.1964)
The Garden c.1987
Derek M. Harte

Victoria Crowe (b.1945)
Coats Behind the Door
Briony Anderson
Editor Scottish Art News, The Fleming Collection

David Abercrombie Donaldson (1916–1996)
Portrait of David Donald, Keeper of Art 1968–1985
Selina Skipwith
Keeper of Art, The Fleming Collection

John Duncan (1866–1945)
The Turn of the Tide
David Horne
Musician, Composer

J.D. Fergusson (1874–1961)
The Drift Posts 1923
Gavin Rochussen
Group Chief Executive Officer, JO Hambro Capital Management Ltd.

Helen Flockart (b.1963)
Canute 1997
David Patterson
Curator, Fine Art Collections, City Art Centre, Edinburgh

Millie Frood (1900–1988)
Workers in the Field
Brian Cox
Actor

Sir Herbert James Gunn (1893–1964)
The Eve of the Battle of the Somme 1916
Little Sparta
Performers of blackened future folk music

Sir Herbert James Gunn (1893–1964)
The Eve of the Battle of the Somme 1916 with
Charles Avery (b.1973) *Untitled*, 2002
Abigail Docherty
Playwright and author of *Molly and John* a short play performed by The Clamjamfry Company at The Fleming Collection in 2007. It was about a soldier's last day with his family before going into battle, where the calm of Gunn's painting will be destroyed, and the unspoken words in Avery's are lost forever.

George Henry (1858–1943)
Girl Reading 1896
Adam Fleming
Chairman, Fleming Family and Partners

Peter Howson (b.1958)
Road Sweeper
Tim Cornwell
Arts Correspondent, The Scotsman

Ian Hughes (1958)
Franz Kafka 1992
John Wallace
Principal, Royal Scottish Academy of Music and Drama

Sir John Lavery (1856–1941)
The Blue Hungarians 1888
Andrew Patrick
Former Managing Director of The Fine Art Society, London, Collector

Charles Rennie Mackintosh (1868–1928)
Butterfly Flower, Bowling 1912
Anna Meredith
Musician, Composer, Teacher, Animateur

Alexander Nasmyth (1758–1840)
A Stormy Highland Scene
Sandi Thom
Singer, Songwriter

Brian Nicol (b.1948)
The Survivors or Journey Survivors
Dominic Hill
Artistic Director, Traverse Theatre, Edinburgh

John Watson Nicol (1856–1926)
'Lochaber No More' 1883
Hannah Peel
Musician, Curator. A live installation performance piece inspired by this painting with traditional music arranged and performed by Hannah Peel and The Clamjamfry Company at The Fleming Collection in 2007 (featuring the voice of Ewan Downie).

John Watson Nicol (1856–1926)
'Lochaber No More' 1883
Robin Fleming, Chairman of the Trustees
The Fleming-Wyfold Art Foundation

Waller Hugh Paton (1828–1895)
Craigmillar Castle 1861
Paul Roberts
Vice Chairman, Lyon & Turnbull Auctioneers

S.J. Peploe (1871–1935)
Green Sea, Iona c.1920
Ewan Mundy
Director of Ewan Mundy Fine Art Ltd, Glasgow

S.J. Peploe (1871–1935)
A Vase of Pink Roses c.1925
William Packer
Freelance Arts Writer

James Ferrier Pryde (1866–1941)
The Unknown Corner 1912
Bill Smith
Director at Flemings and Keeper of Art from 1985 to 1997; Trustee, The Fleming-Wyfold Art Foundation

James Ferrier Pryde (1866–1941)
The Unknown Corner 1912
Merlin James
Artist, Writer

Anne Redpath (1895–1965)
Houses on a Hill c.1958
Carole Warren
Collector

Anne Redpath (1895–1965)
Houses on a Hill c.1958
Patrick Bourne
Managing Director, The Fine Art Society, London

Philip Reeves (b.1931)
Vapour Trail over the Hill 1973
Alasdair Nicolson
Composer and Director of St Magnus Composers

William Simpson (1823–1899)
The Great Banyan Tree, Botanic Gardens, Calcutta 1859
Laura Lindsay
Director, Christie's

Edward Arthur Walton (1860–1922)
The Ale Water
Andre Zlattinger
Former Head of Scottish Art, Sotheby's

ACKNOWLEDGEMENTS

Supporters of The Fleming Collection

Founder Members
Fleming Family & Partners Ltd

Corporate Members
Evercore Partners Ltd
Eton College
Flemings Hotel, Mayfair
RFIB Group Ltd
Ridgeway Partners LLP
others wishing to remain anonymous

Other Supporters
Patrons of The Fleming-Wyfold Art Foundation
Philanthropic Friends and
Friends of The Fleming Collection
Lyon & Turnbull, Sponsors of Scottish Art News

We would also like to thank Caroline Pile and Sue Pile of Piledrivers, Catherine Hammond of Flemings Hotel, Mayfair, Mark Tilley and Matthew Blythe of Palette Events, Alex Hewitt of The Scotsman and Briony Anderson, Evelyn Gladstone, Lucy Lyell and Rebecca Mundy at The Fleming Collection.

The Fleming-Wyfold Art Foundation's acquisitions and activities are funded entirely by grants and donations from charitable foundations, companies and private individuals and receives no public funding.

FF&P

FLEMINGS
MAYFAIR

THE SCOTSMAN